RISE UP

WRITTEN BY AMANDA LI

ILLUSTRATED BY AMY BLACKWELL

EDITED BY IMOGEN WILLIAMS
DESIGNED BY KIM HANKINSON AND JACK CLUCAS

Buster Books

CONTENTS

INTRODUCTION

Is there something you've always dreamed of doing but feared it might be impossible? Do you ever wonder how you'd cope if you found yourself in danger?

Discover the incredible true stories of girls and boys from around the world who have overcome the challenges facing them. They have survived shark attacks, climbed mountains and escaped avalanches. They are environmentalists, activists and inventors, who are all changing the world, one step at a time.

Explore the skills and advice that could help you follow in their footsteps and navigate through your own challenges. Learn how to survive extreme circumstances and discover tips for getting your voice heard.

Get ready to meet the daredevils, dreamers and doers who weren't afraid to rise up and achieve their dreams, and be inspired to share your own story with the world.

· ·

'AN INSPIRATIONAL BOOK TELLING THE TALES OF 29 AMAZING CHILDREN. CHILDREN WHO HAVE TRIUMPHED, OVERCOME AND PERSEVERED. CHILDREN WHO WOULD PUT MOST GROWN-UPS TO SHAME!' – KONNIE HUQ

THE GUTSY TALE OF
GRETA THUNBERG

SWEDEN

Greta shifted around, trying to get comfortable on the hard ground. The cobblestones underneath her were cold and rough. People walked by, looking down at her, then glancing at her home-made sign. She had been sitting here alone, outside the Swedish Parliament building, for six hours.

IT WAS NEARLY TIME TO LEAVE, BUT SHE WOULD BE BACK AGAIN SOON.

It was Friday 20th August, 2018. Greta promised herself that she would sit here every single Friday from now on, come rain or shine. She would never give up because there was too much at stake. The future of the Earth was in peril – she couldn't let climate change be ignored anymore.

When she was eight years old, Greta Thunberg learned about climate change and wondered why more wasn't being done about it. Greta and her family did their best to recycle their rubbish, they were conscious of not wasting water and they tried to cycle instead of drive. Greta even became a vegan to try and reduce her personal impact on climate change.

Then, in the summer of 2018, a scorching heatwave hit Europe and devastating forest fires broke out in Sweden. It was impossible for Greta to overlook this. She knew it had happened because of climate change. Greta was 15 and she realized she had to do something more – for her generation, and for all generations to come.

SO, SHE DECIDED TO GO ON STRIKE.

She painted a sign on a piece of wood that said 'Skolstrejk För Klimatet' – 'School Strike For Climate'. Instead of going to school that day, Greta cycled to the Parliament building and sat down outside. She would make her voice heard. She would make the government and the big companies take notice of her and take urgent action against climate change.

That first day, Greta sat alone. On the second day, a few people joined her.

SINCE THEN, GRETA HAS NEVER BEEN ALONE.

Gradually, thousands of school children from more than a hundred countries around the world have joined her, holding their own climate strikes on Fridays.

Greta had started a movement, now known as 'Fridays For The Future'. She has appeared on TV, and spread her ideas by giving TED talks and by speaking at important world events, such as the United Nations Climate Change Conference.

This is even more of an achievement for Greta, as she has Asperger syndrome and often finds it difficult to communicate with other people. But she doesn't let this get in the way of her goals. She knows that stopping the effects of climate change is the most important thing in the world. Greta's message is clear: This is the greatest threat that humankind has ever faced, and we need to take action – now.

WHAT CAN YOU DO?

HERE ARE SOME SMALL CHANGES THAT MAKE A BIG DIFFERENCE:

- Don't use a car for short trips. Walk instead. You'll be fitter and it will help the environment at the same time.

- Always turn the light off when leaving a room.

- Don't leave TVs and computers on standby. Switch them off at the mains.

- Recycle everything you can and try not to buy things with lots of packaging.

- To save water, turn off the taps when brushing your teeth. Take showers, and fewer baths.

- Buy and use less stuff. Ask yourself if you really need something before you buy it.

- Eat less meat. The farming of animals contributes to climate change. Replace some of your meals with vegan alternatives – such as oat milk and soya mince.

WHAT IS CLIMATE CHANGE?

- Our planet is slowly heating up. The changing climate is making our weather much more extreme. As temperatures rise, some parts of the world are getting wetter, while others are getting hotter and have droughts.

- Trees and plants absorb carbon dioxide. When forests are cut down for wood and other products, we have fewer trees to get rid of the carbon dioxide.

- Climate change is mostly caused by humans. Our cars, planes, homes, factories and farms use fuel and release gases that trap heat from the sun.

- If climate change continues, it will continue to have very serious affects on the future of animals, plants and humans.

HOW TO BE AN ENVIRONMENTAL ACTIVIST

1. **Get informed.** Find out as much as you can about climate change, its causes and its effects. Why not start an eco-club at school or with friends?

2. **Give your time to the cause.** Volunteer and help out in any way you can.

3. **Make your voice heard.** Sharing your views could help to change other people's attitudes.

4. **Don't give up.** It can take a long time to make a difference but it will be worth it. Every little helps!

XIUHTEZCATL MARTINEZ

> USA

Xiuhtezcatl Martinez was taught from an early age that protecting the Earth is everyone's responsibility. He has made it his mission to share these views and uses rap as a way to make his voice heard. He is the Youth Director for Earth Guardians, a group of activists, artists and musicians from around the world who work together to make change happen in their communities. Hip-hop artist, activist, voice for his generation, Xiuhtezcatl Martinez is changing the world, little by little, every day, whether performing hip-hop at music festivals or speaking at rallies.

THE INVENTIVE IDEAS OF
WILLIAM KAMKWAMBA

MALAWI

William balanced on top of the tower that he had built from wood and bamboo. It was a strange-looking contraption. It had an old bicycle wheel attached to the top, a large fan alongside it and various other machine parts. A gust of wind blew and the fan's blades began spinning around. William held up a light bulb that was attached to the machinery. The bulb flickered and died. Then it lit up brightly.

"He's made light!" shouted the crowd, which had gathered below to watch this crazy boy. They were right. William had made electricity. But how?

A few months before, 14-year-old William Kamkwamba had been sitting in the library, trying not to think about how hungry he was. This wasn't an everyday kind of hunger – this was starvation. The maize harvest had failed in Malawi that year and there was hardly anything to eat. People were starving, selling anything they could just to buy a few grains. Nobody had food or much money. William went to the library to learn because his family could not afford to pay his school fees.

A book called *Using Energy* caught William's eye. He'd always been interested in how things worked and had spent hours fixing old radios. On the book's cover was a picture of tall, grey towers with large, spinning blades. William was intrigued. He flipped through the pages to find out more. These machines were called wind turbines and they used the energy from wind to make power. This was exciting! If William had a windmill,

"HE'S MADE LIGHT!"
SHOUTED THE CROWD.

maybe he could make electricity to light the dark nights in Malawi. He might be able to pump water to the fields to help to grow the crops. Electricity would be the answer to many of his family's problems.

William set to work straight away. He knew what he wanted to make, but finding the right materials was difficult when there were only bits of scrap around. He used lots of different things: a washing line, an old bicycle frame, plastic pipes. William heated and flattened the pipes, then cut them into blades for the windmill.

It took him a long time to gather everything he needed but, after several months of hard work, he had finally built his windmill.

THE MOMENT WHEN HE PRODUCED LIGHT FOR THE FIRST TIME WAS INCREDIBLE!

The windmill was able to power four lights and two radios in his family home. Soon, everyone in the village wanted one.

William's windmill got him a lot of attention. He was invited to speak at a TED conference about his idea – and about his dreams of building a bigger windmill to help the village. His speech was a great success and he got lots of help and advice from the people he met at the conference.

Since then, William has been working on many projects for his area. Lots of them are sustainable, including solar power and lighting for several homes, a deep-water well with a solar-powered pump for clean water and an irrigation system for crops. William is full of bright ideas. His inventive thinking shows that something huge can be achieved from very little.

WHERE IS HE NOW?

William's story is told in his book, and the film of the same name, *The Boy Who Harnessed the Wind*. He is now working on a project that encourages young people to follow in his footsteps and create something practical to improve their lives and that of their community.

HOW TO BE AN INVENTOR

1. Look at the world around you and find a problem that needs solving.

2. Be creative! Use your imagination to think differently about the way things work.

3. Keep a book in which to make notes and sketches of your ideas.

4. Make a prototype. This is a working model of your idea.

5. Test your idea out. Ask family and friends what they think.

6. Make your product! Do some research and ask an adult to help you to contact companies that might be interested in producing it.

GREEN MEASURES IN YOUR OWN HOME

Here are some simple things you can
do to be more environmentally friendly.

- **Use less water.** Take shorter showers and definitely don't leave the water running while you brush your teeth.

- **Think about how you get around.** If you can, walk or cycle to where you need to be. If you need to use transport, get a bus or share the car journey with friends.

- **Remember to save electricity whenever you can.** Turn lights off when you leave the room and use energy-efficient modes on your devices.

ANN MAKOSINSKI

CANADA

Ann Makosinski invented a thermoelectric torch when she was just 15 years old. The light is powered by the heat of the hand that holds it. She was inspired to create it after hearing that a friend in the Philippines was struggling to study because she couldn't afford to pay for electricity after it got dark in the evening.

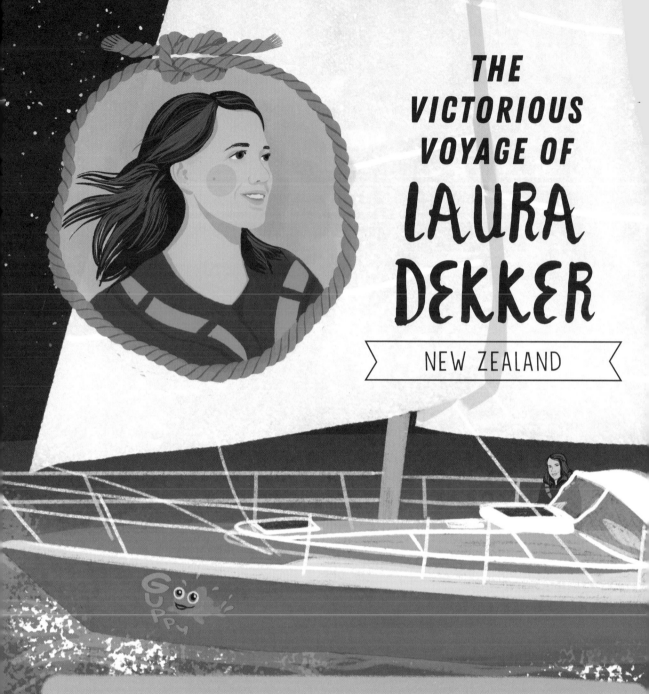

THE VICTORIOUS VOYAGE OF LAURA DEKKER

NEW ZEALAND

Laura's sailing boat, *Guppy*, looked tiny as it was tossed around on the increasingly stormy waves. The wind was howling and screeching. Inside the cabin, Laura was trying to decide what to do. As water smashed against the portholes, she shuddered. Suddenly, there was a huge crash and Laura was flung across the cabin into a table. Cupboard doors flew open and bowls rolled across the floor. Swirling, foaming water filled the boat as a giant wave came down on top of *Guppy*. Laura managed to pull herself up and get on to the deck. She needed to

'reef' the sail – which would make it smaller and slow the boat down. Soaked through, she lurched across the deck and fumbled with freezing hands to roll up the sail. She would not be sleeping tonight.

Laura Dekker was sailing around the Cape of Good Hope in South Africa. She was completely alone and only 16 years old. She'd had many alarming experiences during her long voyage. A huge whale almost overturned her boat, *Guppy* had near-collisions with massive cargo ships on more than one occasion, and its sails were often ripped up by the high winds – not to mention the times she was hit by waves up to 8 metres high.

And it was lonely. At times, Laura's only companions were the cockroaches living on *Guppy* and the flying fish that landed every so often on the deck. The special moments made up for it though: being followed by pods of lively dolphins jumping out of the water, watching the most beautiful sunsets over the ocean and arriving at each new destination to be greeted by supporters and friends.

Laura Dekker was just eight when she decided her ambition was to sail around the world. Over the next few years, her dad taught her everything he knew about sailing, from ocean navigation to working out wind directions. Laura had many practice

SHE WAS COMPLETELY ALONE AND ONLY 16 YEARS OLD.

voyages and learnt first aid in case she got injured. She was used to surviving on just one or two hours of sleep on long-distance journeys. By 13, Laura had already made a solo voyage from the Netherlands, where she lived, to England.

Now, Laura was ready to plan her big adventure. Her round-the-world route would take her to the Caribbean island of St. Maarten, then across the Pacific, Indian and Atlantic Oceans, to arrive back at St. Maarten 27,000 nautical miles (50,000 kilometres) later. She would stop at different places along the way to get food and water supplies and to contact her family. On 21st August, 2010, Laura left Gibraltar and sailed to the Canary Islands to begin the Atlantic crossing to St. Maarten.

One year and five months later, Laura sailed triumphantly back into the harbour at St. Maarten. She was accompanied by a group of boats cheering her on – one was driven by her delighted mum and dad. Laura waved to the crowds of cheering fans. She'd done it. Laura Dekker was now one of the youngest people to circumnavigate the world solo by boat. What an achievement!

HOW TO TIE A REEF KNOT

The reef knot is a sailor's knot that is often used to tie down part of a sail during reefing – rolling the edge of a sail up to make it smaller. Here's how to tie it:

1. Take two pieces of rope. Take the right end (blue) and place it over the left end (orange). Then bring it under the left rope.

2. Next, cross the left end over the right end, above the twist.

3. Bring the left end under the right.

4. Pull the ends firmly to make the knot tight.

EMERGENCY!

IF THINGS GO WRONG ON THE WATER, HERE IS SOME ADVICE FOR WHAT TO DO:

- Send a 'Mayday' message by radio or satellite phone. You can't rely on a mobile phone at sea.

- Send an SOS (Save Our Souls) message – this uses a system of dots and dashes called Morse Code. An SOS is three dots, three dashes, three dots. You can signal with sound, torches, flashlights or mirrors.

- Activate your Personal Locator Beacon (PLB) – an electronic transmitter which alerts rescuers to your location if you're in danger.

- Set off an emergency flare – a device that shoots up into the sky producing a bright light or coloured smoke.

- Hoist your emergency flag – sailors have special flags that they use to communicate with.

HOW TO SEND A 'MAYDAY' MESSAGE

1. Press the red distress button on your radio.

2. Speak loudly, slowly and clearly.

3. Say "Mayday, Mayday, Mayday. This is [name of your boat. Say this three times]. Mayday."

4. Explain your location and describe your emergency.

5. Say "Over" to show that you have finished the message and let go of the button.

TRAVEL PLANNING

If you're planning a voyage, you need to be prepared.

- Pack plenty of water.

- Take emergency food supplies that will last you at least 24 hours.

- Make sure you have somewhere warm and dry to sleep.

- Take a map and a detailed plan of your route.

- Always tell someone where you're going and leave a copy of your route with them in case of emergency.

THE DRAMATIC DANCING OF
JOEL KIOKO

KENYA

Joel stood at the back of the hall and watched the ballet dancers performing their show for his school. It seemed a very strange kind of dancing to him. He had never seen anything like it before in Kenya. But he liked the way the dancers leaped and jumped high into the air, like graceful athletes. Joel had always been good at somersaults and high jumps, so he thought he might like to give ballet a try. His friends laughed at him, but Joel ignored them and signed up for the free class.

Three years later, at the age of 13, Joel was practising turns and spins in his regular ballet class. There was no ballet

HE LIKED THE WAY THE DANCERS LEAPED AND JUMPED HIGH INTO THE AIR, LIKE GRACEFUL ATHLETES.

barre or mirror – just a shabby, empty classroom – but Joel didn't mind. He was used to not having much space.

Joel lived with his mother, sister, aunt and grandmother in a small shack in the dusty Kuwinda slums of Nairobi. People here struggled to make a living and Joel didn't know anybody who wanted to be a dancer. Sometimes his friends teased him about his hobby, but he didn't care. Ballet was his life now, something that he was really good at. It made him feel proud.

One day, Joel noticed a girl enter the room. He carried on trying as hard as he could to perform a perfect grand jeté – a high jump that was almost like doing the splits in the air. The girl was impressed. Who was this boy who could jump so high? She told her ballet teacher, Cooper Rust, about the talented young man she had spotted. When she saw Joel for herself, Cooper agreed with her – and decided to help Joel as much as she could.

With Cooper's encouragement – and lots of hard work – Joel passed his ballet exams with top marks and was taken on by a ballet school in the USA for three months of special training. He also got his first taste of the theatre – a leading role in *The Nutcracker* ballet at the Kenya National Theatre.

Joel is now Kenya's most promising young ballet dancer.

HE HAS BECOME QUITE FAMOUS FOR HIS AMAZINGLY HIGH JUMPS, WHICH SEEM TO DEFY GRAVITY.

By the time he was 17, he had won a scholarship to the English National Ballet School in London, one of the most respected dance schools in the world. Joel is on track to become a professional dancer, but however famous he becomes, he knows one thing – he will never forget where he came from.

WHERE IS HE NOW?

Joel's dream is to become a professional ballet dancer and perform all over the world. He would like to open a studio in Nairobi so that he can teach other children like him how to dance.

SPIN WITHOUT GETTING DIZZY

**Have you ever wondered how dancers spin around without feeling dizzy?
They do something called 'spotting'. Here's how:**

1. Stand up straight and look ahead.

2. Pick a spot or object at eye level in front of you and focus on it.

3. As your body moves around, keep looking at the same spot until you can't turn any more. Then, turn your head quickly so it returns to its starting point. You should be looking at the same spot again. This helps to keep you stable and stops the dizziness.

4. Practise! The more you do it, the easier it gets. With lots of practice, some dancers can do one spin after another, without feeling dizzy at all.

HOW TO BUILD UP YOUR STRENGTH AND FITNESS

- **Squats.** Stand with your feet shoulder-width apart and stretch your arms out in front of you. Keep your back straight and bend your knees until they are nearly at a right angle and then stand up straight again.

- **Walking.** Brisk walking stimulates your heart, lungs and circulation, known as your cardiovascular system.

- **Lunges.** Stand with your feet hip-width apart. Slowly bend your knees and extend your right leg so your knee nearly touches the floor. Then push up to standing and repeat with your left leg.

- **Plank.** Lie on your front, balancing on your toes and hands. You can lean on your elbows instead if you prefer. Keep your legs and back straight and hold this position for ten seconds, then rest and repeat ten times.

- **Star jumps.** Stand up tall with your legs together and arms by your side. Then jump in the air and extend your arms and legs into a star shape, before bringing your legs and arms back together when you land.

POORNA FELT SO TIRED AND WEAK. HOW WOULD SHE FIND THE ENERGY TO KEEP CLIMBING?

THE DIZZY HEIGHTS OF
POORNA MALAVATH

INDIA

Everest – the highest mountain in the world. Poorna was so close to the summit. There was just one obstacle left – Summit Ridge. A huge crest of snow, it was dangerously steep with a terrifying 3,000-metre drop on both sides. Poorna felt so tired and weak. How would she find the energy to keep climbing? As she looked up at the challenge ahead, something caught her eye at the side of the ridge. It looked like a person lying in the snow. Poorna stopped in her tracks. It *was* a person.

Poorna knew how dangerous Everest was but seeing this reminded her how tough it was going to be. That person was a climber who hadn't made it. They had been left there, frozen in the ice, because there was no way to get a body down from a deadly mountain. Poorna had to be very brave and remind herself why she was doing this. She wanted to prove that girls could do anything – and she wouldn't give up now. Poorna took a deep breath and continued onwards – and upwards.

It is hard to believe that Poorna hadn't done much climbing as a child. She was the daughter of poor farm workers who lived in a small village in Telangana, India. Usually, girls like her would not get the chance to go climbing. But Poorna had been lucky – she was chosen to take part in the expedition while she was at school. From that moment on, she did everything she could to meet the challenges of climbing Everest. And there were lots of them. Winds on the mountain can reach over 280 kilometres per hour and temperatures can get a low as minus 60 degrees Celsius.

The moment when she finally made it to the summit was incredible. After five weeks of slow, painful ascent, here she was, standing at the top of the world. It was 25th May, 2014, and Poorna Malavath had just become the youngest girl to climb Everest, at the age of 13 years and 11 months. She hoisted the Indian national flag that she had brought with her, feeling so proud to see it flying on top of Everest. But she couldn't spend too long up there. Fifteen minutes later, the team had to start their descent.

Everyone knew that coming down was even more dangerous than going up. However, Poorna was well-prepared. She and her teammate had done eight months of hard training in the mountains to prepare themselves. Getting used to the lack of oxygen at high altitude was especially hard. They were 8,848 metres above sea level and Poorna had vomited most days while her body adapted to the mountain air. The packet food she was given during the expedition also made her sick.

Despite all of these challenges, Poorna achieved her dream. Her willpower and endurance have earned her a place in the record books, proving that girls really can do anything.

EVEREST DANGERS

ALMOST 300 CLIMBERS HAVE DIED ON EVEREST. RISKS INCLUDE:

- Being swept away by an avalanche
- Falling into a deep, icy crevasse
- Getting caught in a sudden snowstorm
- Getting hypothermia – when your body temperature drops due to the cold
- Altitude sickness – at these heights it can be fatal

HOW TO PERFORM AN ICE-AXE SELF-ARREST

If you fall over on a mountain, an ice-axe self-arrest will stop you from sliding down the slope.

- Always have your ice axe close to hand in case you fall. Grasp the axe like a walking stick, with the pick facing backwards while you walk.

- Don't have your ice axe strapped to your backpack – you won't be able to reach it in an emergency.

- If you fall, turn on to your back with your feet pointing downhill. Act quickly, as the longer you wait, the faster you will accelerate downhill and the harder it will be to stop.

- Stick the pick of your ice axe into the snow just above your shoulder. At the same time, roll on to your front so you are above the axe.

- Hold on to the head of your ice axe and pull your body up towards it.

- If you arch your back and lift your tummy off the snow, you will put more weight on the ice axe, making it easier to stop you falling.

ALTITUDE SICKNESS

THE SYMPTOMS:

- Headache
- Dizziness
- Nausea and vomiting
- Tiredness
- Shortness of breath
- Loss of appetite

HOW TO AVOID IT:

- Take your time. Going too high too fast may make you feel ill, so it's best to keep at a slow, steady pace from the start.

- If you start to feel unwell, take a break until you feel better.

- If you start to feel any symptoms, you should descend the mountain by at least 500 metres until the symptoms pass. If you can walk in a straight line, you can continue your ascent. If not, you should make your way further down the mountain.

THE CREATIVE THINKING OF
BOYAN SLAT

NETHERLANDS

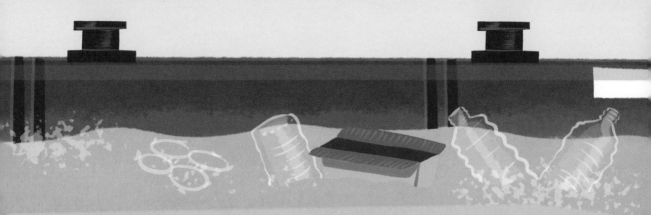

The blue sea sparkled in the Greek sunshine. Sixteen-year-old Boyan Slat was on his summer holidays and having a great time. He adjusted his diving mask, gave his oxygen tank one last check and jumped off the boat with a loud splash. He was looking forward to exploring the underwater world. Maybe he'd be lucky and spot an octopus.

Twenty minutes later, Boyan was not enjoying himself as much as he had expected. Yes, there were some lovely fish swimming around but mostly there were old carrier bags and plastic bottles – hundreds of them, floating in the sea after they had been thrown away. Boyan felt himself getting angry. Why were people dumping so much plastic into the oceans? What would happen to all the sea creatures if this carried on?

When he returned home to the Netherlands, Boyan decided to find out what was being done about this problem. He soon realized. Nothing. No one was trying to get the rubbish out of the sea.

Boyan knew that if he didn't do something, the oceans would one day be completely filled with plastic. He'd always been good at coming up with solutions to problems, but this was a huge challenge. Boyan thought about all the different ways of getting the plastic out of the sea.

Nets would catch sea creatures as well as plastic, so they were no good. Machines would damage the environment through using fuel.

THEN IT CAME TO HIM. WHY NOT USE THE POWER OF THE SEA ITSELF?

Excitedly, Boyan began sketching a design, something that would collect the plastic without harming the environment. He came up with a brilliant invention, which he called The Ocean Cleanup.

It is a system of floating tube-like barriers with a huge skirt that catches all the plastic floating near the surface of the water. The skirt is specially anchored so that it

moves along with the sea currents, but more slowly than the pieces of plastic. This ensures it catches more rubbish. Sea creatures can swim safely underneath it. When full, the plastic can be collected and recycled.

Boyan raised money through a crowdfunding campaign to get his invention off the ground. It has taken years of hard work but Boyan has worked tirelessly to protect the ocean. His dream is that in just five years his invention might be able to get rid of almost half the Great Pacific Garbage Patch. This is a huge area of rubbish, mostly plastic, in the Pacific Ocean between Hawaii and California – it is double the size of Texas.

Boyan's idea generated huge excitement and it was selected as one of the top 25 best inventions of 2015 by *Time* magazine. Boyan also received the Champions of the Earth award from the United Nations Environment Programme. He has gone on to win many more awards – but for Boyan, the most important thing has always been to get rid of the plastic. And with his bright idea, it could be sooner than we think.

FOR BOYAN, THE MOST IMPORTANT THING HAS ALWAYS BEEN TO GET RID OF THE PLASTIC.

THE PLASTIC PROBLEM

- Every year about eight million tonnes of plastic enters our oceans.

- Some pieces float on the surface of the sea, preventing sunlight from reaching the plankton and algae below. If these plants die, so will the sea creatures that eat them.

- Plastics release harmful chemicals as they break down in the water. These can be absorbed by animals and by humans.

- Many sea creatures, such as turtles and whales, swallow plastic bags because they mistake them for food. A whale found in Indonesia had over 1,000 pieces of plastic in its stomach, weighing almost six kilograms. It had eaten more than 100 plastic cups and even a pair of flip-flops.

YOU CAN HELP!

Here are some simple things we can all do to help solve the plastic problem:

- Don't buy drinks in throwaway plastic bottles – get a reusable drinks bottle and refill it instead.

- Don't use plastic drinking straws.

- Avoid plastic carrier bags – take a reusable bag when shopping.

- Keep food in reusable lunch boxes instead of plastic sandwich bags.

- If you see plastic littering a beach, pick it up and put it in the bin.

- Never throw rubbish into the sea or rivers.

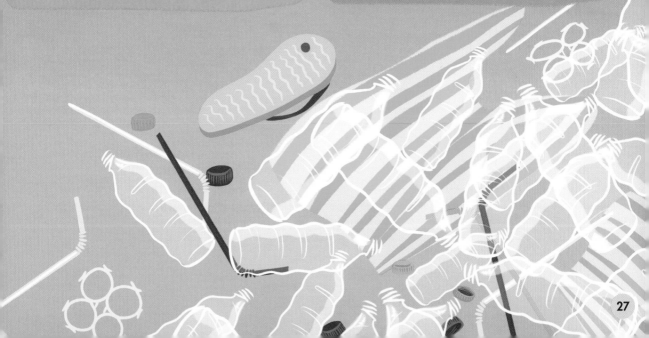

THE TERRIFYING TALE OF
YEONMI PARK

NORTH KOREA

"Run!" the man whispered urgently as he sprinted towards the river. Yeonmi was frozen with fear. She couldn't move her legs. The man looked behind him, stopped, then ran back to grab Yeonmi and her mother. Together, they reached the river and edged out across its frozen surface. Yeonmi couldn't look down. What if the ice beneath them broke? If they fell into the freezing water, they could die. But that wasn't the only danger. There were armed guards along the river and they were ready to shoot anyone who tried to cross it.

When they finally made it to the other side, Yeonmi was so relieved. At last, there was solid land under her feet. But they were not out of danger yet. The three of them ran, as fast as they could, all the while wondering if they would hear shots being fired at them. They didn't stop until they were sure the guards couldn't see them. Yeonmi and her mother had made it to China – but this was just the start of their long, hard journey.

YEONMI PARK WAS 13 WHEN SHE ESCAPED FROM NORTH KOREA.

She and her family paid a man, known as a people smuggler, to help them cross the Yalu river into China one cold, dark night in March 2007.

Yeonmi and her relatives were very unhappy in North Korea. Life had always been hard, but from 1990 onwards there had been a famine and people everywhere were starving. Some were dying. Yeonmi's family, like many others, had to eat insects, tree bark and grass to stay alive, with an occasional treat of a frozen potato or a little bit of rice. But it wasn't just the lack of food. There was no running water and the electricity often went off. People were not allowed to have the Internet or to contact anyone

> **"WE AREN'T FREE TO SING, SAY, WEAR OR THINK WHAT WE WANT."**

outside North Korea. If you criticized the country's leaders, or tried to leave North Korea, you would be severely punished, maybe killed. Yeonmi learnt from a young age never to say what she really thought. "We aren't free to sing, say, wear or think what we want," she later explained to the United Nations.

Yeonmi and her mother spent two years in China and eventually got to South Korea,

where they made a home for themselves. Yeonmi's life is now very different. She has food to eat and she has her freedom. But she has never forgotten the people that she left behind in North Korea, who live such hard lives.

WHERE IS SHE NOW?

Yeonmi is now in her twenties and is studying in New York, USA. She is a human rights activist who uses her voice to let people know about life in North Korea. She has written a book about her experiences.

HOW TO NAVIGATE

If you need to navigate in the wild, you can use a wristwatch and the sun to work out which way is north. The sun sets in the west wherever you are in the world, but in the Northern Hemisphere the sun is due south at 12 noon and in the Southern Hemisphere it is due north at 12 noon.

TO FIND SOUTH IN THE NORTHERN HEMISPHERE:

1. Hold your watch so it is horizontal to the ground and aim the hour hand directly at the sun.

2. The point on the watch face in the middle of the hour hand and 12 noon is due south.

TO FIND NORTH IN THE SOUTHERN HEMISPHERE:

Do exactly the same as above, but instead of showing you which way is south, it will work out which way is north.

HYPOTHERMIA

If you fall into freezing water and your body temperature drops, you may get hypothermia. This can be fatal.

WHAT TO DO:

1. Get inside or find something to protect yourself from the cold ground, like a towel.

2. Take off your wet clothes and get dry.

3. Wrap yourself in blankets or warm clothes.

4. Have a hot drink and something sugary to eat.

5. It is always good to get checked over by a doctor. In an emergency, call an ambulance.

SIGNS ARE:

- Shivering
- Tiredness
- Pale, cold skin
- Being confused
- Slurred speech
- Fast breathing

THE SELFLESS STRUGGLE OF
ABRAHAM KEITA

LIBERIA

Life had always been tough for Abraham. He and his family lived in West Point, one of the biggest slums in Liberia, West Africa. There was little food, no running water or electricity and it was hard to make a living. Abraham's dad worked as a driver and managed to keep the family going. That morning, he had left for work as usual. Later, the family received shocking news. His car had been attacked and he had been killed.

Abraham was five years old on the day that his father died. His family were devastated. They thought the world had turned against them and they lost all hope for the future. Abraham's mother was left to look after him and his siblings without any money. Life became so hard and a matter of just trying to survive each day.

By the time Abraham was nine years old, he had seen and heard many terrible things. Violent acts occurred every day in Liberia. One of the poorest countries in the world, Liberia was also in the midst of a war. The violence was not just happening to adults. Some children were being forced to fight as soldiers in the conflict. Others had lost their parents and were living on the dangerous, crime-ridden streets.

When Abraham heard that a 13-year-old girl in his neighbourhood had been killed, he knew he had to do something. *She could have been my sister,* he thought. Abraham joined a march to protest about violence against children. He was angry. Why should children have to suffer at the hands of adults?

It felt good to shout and let the world know about his anger and sense of injustice. After taking part in the peaceful protest, and making an impression on his peers, Abraham was invited to join the Liberian Children's Parliament, where his passion for advocacy was nurtured.

Abraham didn't stop there. He carried on going to marches and speaking about violence against children. In September 2011, he organized a big protest and got 200 children to take part. Together they demanded that the government of Liberia pass a new law to protect and respect the rights of children. The lawmakers listened and, in 2012, Liberia became one of the first African countries to have a children's rights law. It was an amazing achievement, especially for a 14-year-old.

Since then, Abraham has continued his activism. He has been called a 'changemaker' – a person who changes the world for the better. He has spoken in different countries, led demonstrations and campaigned for an end to violence against children in the world. At 17, he was incredibly proud to be awarded the 2015 International Children's Peace Prize, one of the top awards for young peace activists.

Abraham believes that, however difficult one's childhood, it is possible to change your life and to help others. He is an incredible young man who stands up and speaks for children everywhere. He wants everyone to remember that children are human beings too, and their rights need to be respected.

KNOW YOUR RIGHTS

Every child should expect some basic things from life. However, many children around the world do not have all these things. The United Nations (UN) Convention on the Rights of the Child says that all children are entitled to:

EDUCATION

HEALTH

LIFE AND SURVIVAL

THE OPPORTUNITY TO PLAY

PROTECTION FROM ABUSE, VIOLENCE AND NEGLECT

BE A CHANGEMAKER

Any action, however small, is a start. If you believe in what you are doing, you can dream big. Here are some tips to get you started:

- Do you have an idea that could make your school, your community or even the world a better place? Share it and let others know.

- Why not volunteer at school or a local kids' club? You can help the younger kids to read, play sports, learn about the environment —

or do whatever you love or are passionate about.

- Why not try fundraising? There are lots of fun and creative ways to raise money. For example, you could run a race where you are sponsored by friends and family for a cause you want to support. Or you could have a bake sale.

THE SURVIVAL STORY OF
JULIANE KOEPCKE

GERMANY

Juliane slowly opened her eyes. Above her all she could see were tree branches. She could hear birds chirping, insects buzzing and the howls of monkeys. Where on earth was she?

Then Juliane remembered. She recalled being on a plane, a flash of lightning and a loud bang. Passengers were screaming and luggage was flying everywhere. Then they were falling ... falling through the sky.

Now she was lying on the ground, still strapped into her passenger seat, which had been completely ripped out of the plane. Her neck hurt, but she forced herself to get out of the seat and stand up. She was in the middle of a rainforest.

"Help," she called out, weakly. No one replied. Juliane had never felt more alone.

Hours later, there was a loud engine sound overhead. A rescue plane! Juliane shouted and screamed for help. But the noise soon faded and Juliane realized the terrible truth – rescuers would never be able to spot her through the thick foliage. She would die if she stayed where she was.

SO JULIANE DECIDED TO WALK HER WAY OUT OF THE RAINFOREST.

What happened to Juliane Koepcke is one of the most amazing survival stories ever known. She was only 17 when the plane she was travelling on with her mother was hit by a storm and crashed into the

SHE WOULD DIE IF SHE STAYED WHERE SHE WAS.

Peruvian rainforest. It was Christmas Eve, 1971. Juliane fell more than 3,000 metres from the plane and survived. When she awoke, she was wearing only a thin dress, one sandal and had lost her glasses. The only food she had was a bag of sweets. She was badly injured but her only thought was that she had to get to safety. She managed to make the sweets last for four days, but when she finished them, she became increasingly desperate to find help.

Juliane and her parents, who were from Germany originally, had lived in Peru for a while, so she knew a lot about the rainforest. She understood that finding water was vital, so when she came across a stream, she followed it.

She waded through the water in a downstream direction, hoping that this might lead her to people. She was also able to drink flowing water from the stream.

FOR TEN LONG DAYS, JULIANE WALKED AND WALKED.

Finally, she found a small path by the river that led up to a hut. She went in but no one was there, so she collapsed and went to sleep. The next day, she found gasoline outside and she poured it on to one of her wounds that was infested with maggots to clean it. She stayed in the hut for the rest of the day. Early in the evening, she heard voices approaching – some forest workers had come to the hut. She had found help. Poor Juliane was in a terrible state – her collarbone was broken and she was covered in insect bites and deep cuts. But she had survived – and her incredible story is still told around the world.

FIND WATER!

- Lick drops of dew from leaves.
- Make a water funnel to collect rainwater (see opposite page).
- Don't drink still, dark water as it may make you sick. Try to find a source of fast-flowing water to drink from.
- If the only water you can find is dirty, filter it through a cloth.
- If you find a stream or river, follow it in a downstream direction. People are more likely to live near the water and the river will lead you out of the rainforest.

YOU CAN LIVE FOR MANY DAYS WITHOUT FOOD, BUT NOT WITHOUT WATER.

RAINFOREST SURVIVAL TIPS

Find a long stick. Rainforest plants can sting and prick, so use a stick to push them out of the way. Sticks are also good for breaking up spider webs.

A fire keeps creatures away and you can boil water to make it clean to drink. However, do not depend on being able to light a fire. A rainforest is an incredibly wet place, making fuel hard to burn.

Mosquitoes bite and can carry a dangerous disease called malaria. Make sure you cover up your body as much as possible.

There are lots of fruits and seeds in the rainforest, but some are poisonous. Look out for monkeys and watch what they eat. The chances are you'll be able to eat it too.

HOW TO MAKE A WATER FUNNEL

FOLLOW THESE STEPS TO COLLECT CLEAN DRINKING WATER:

1. Find a large leaf with a stalk.
2. Lean the leaf against a tree at an angle so that dew or rainwater will run down the stalk.
3. Collect the water at the bottom of the 'funnel'.
4. If you don't have a bottle or container, look for anything that will hold water, such as a fruit skin.

THE CALM COURAGE OF

DESMOND DOSS

USA

BOOM! The deafening sound of exploding bomb shells filled the air. A bullet whizzed past Desmond's head. As he ducked down, he spotted a wounded soldier lying nearby. Desmond crawled over and grabbed the man. He needed to carry him to safety and the only way out was 120 metres down a sheer cliff.

HOW WOULD HE GET HIM DOWN?

Desmond remembered a knot he had learned to tie when he was a boy. He grabbed a rope and fastened it securely around the man, then tied the other end around a tree stump. Slowly, Desmond began lowering him down the sheer cliff face. The soldier was heavy, but Desmond somehow found the strength to hold the rope even though it made his hands bleed. Panting and sweating,

Desmond got the man safely down to his comrades, who were gathered at the bottom of the cliff.

It was 5th May, 1945, and Desmond was one of the soldiers making up the troops fighting in Okinawa, Japan. Desmond had always been different from the other soldiers. Because of his religious beliefs, he refused to kill anyone, even in war, and he would not carry a weapon. The other soldiers thought he was a coward who was afraid to fight. But Desmond knew that he should try to save lives, not end them.

Desmond Doss had joined the US Army Medical Corps in 1942, wanting to help in the Second World War. But because he wouldn't harm the opposing side, he was bullied and laughed at by the other soldiers.

On that day in May, the soldiers were in a nightmare situation. Only a handful of them remained uninjured. Desmond could have gone without them, but he couldn't leave those other men to die, even if it meant dying himself. Despite the terrible danger, he wanted to stay. After he had rescued the first man, Desmond ran back into the gunfire to save the others. It took him many hours, but Desmond would not stop. He carried, pulled and hauled every single man down the cliff to safety. He saved 75 men that day and risked his own life, over and over again.

IT WAS AN EXTRAORDINARY ACT OF COURAGE.

His Commanding Officer and comrades completely changed their minds about Desmond and they realized he wasn't a coward after all – he was a hero. On 12th October, 1945, Desmond went to the White House to meet the President of the USA and to receive the Medal of Honour. Desmond had always done what he believed was right – and his bravery was finally rewarded.

DESMOND KNEW THAT HE SHOULD TRY TO SAVE LIVES, NOT END THEM.

HOW TO TIE A
BOWLINE KNOT

1. Make a small loop in the rope.

2. Hold the end of the rope closest to you. Bring it under and through the loop. Then bring it around the back of the upper rope and back through the loop again.

3. Tighten the knot by pulling on the end while holding the upper rope.

HOW TO BE AN EVERYDAY HERO

- **When there are unpopular jobs to do, make sure you chip in and help out.** It shows that you don't think you're too good to do tasks that you expect others to do.

- **Offer your seat to someone who may need it more than you.** If you are on a train or bus and see someone less able to stand than you – for instance someone who is older, pregnant or injured – let them have your seat. People will appreciate your kindness and consideration.

- **You've achieved great things.** You know it. Other people know it. You're the talk of the town. So there's no need to show off and boast. It might feel nice when someone says good things about you, but a real hero doesn't chase praise – they are modest.

THE REMARKABLE TALENT OF

PHIONA MUTESI

UGANDA

A barefoot girl in a ragged dress watched as her older brother left their tiny shack and made his way through the dusty streets of Katwe.

Where was he going? Would there be any food there? She was so hungry. The girl thought she would follow him and find out. She kept well out of sight and was surprised to see him go through a doorway into a small hall. Slipping in after him, she watched as he sat on a bench opposite another boy. On a table between them was a board covered in black and white squares. On the squares were beautiful little carved objects in different colours. The girl had never seen anything like them. She was entranced.

"Hello there," said a smiling man, who was watching the children. "Why don't you come in?"

The girl felt very shy. But she went in and listened to the man, whose name was Robert, as he explained what her brother was doing. He was playing a game called chess. Robert showed her what to do. She picked up a pawn and moved it across the board. From that moment, she knew that chess would be her game.

The girl's name was Phiona Mutesi. She began to attend Robert's chess classes after school, to learn the game and get a bowl of porridge, too. Robert was trying to help the children who lived in the Katwe slums of Uganda, Africa. Their lives were very hard. The slum was dirty, smelly and full of flies and diseases. Every day there was a struggle to find food and water. Phiona was only nine years old, but she'd had to leave school when she was six and she couldn't read or write. But she could certainly play chess.

PHIONA SOON BEGAN WINNING AGAINST THE OTHER CHILDREN IN THE CLASS.

One boy burst into tears when he was beaten by a girl for the first time. Phiona had a natural ability and practised hard. In less than a year, she beat Robert. He realized it was time for Phiona to go out

SHE COULDN'T READ OR WRITE. BUT SHE COULD CERTAINLY PLAY CHESS.

into the world and play chess against the very best.

So that's what she did. At 11 years old, Phiona won the Ugandan Women's Junior Championship. In 2009, she represented Uganda in Africa's International Children's Chess Tournament in Sudan. She was 13 and it was the first time she'd been on a plane. When she got to the hotel, she realized it would be the first time she would have a bed to herself.

With Robert's help, Phiona was able to go back to school. She has since played in three more World Chess Olympiad competitions and now she helps other children to learn the game and be inspired. Chess changed Phiona's life and she is determined to help change the lives of others.

WHERE IS SHE NOW?

Phiona went to college in the USA and she hopes to be a chess Grandmaster one day – the highest level a chess player can reach. Her amazing story has been made into a film and a book.

THE CHESS PIECES AND THEIR MOVES

BISHOP

Can move diagonally any number of squares in any direction.

KNIGHT

Can move in an 'L' shape – two squares forward or back, then one square across – or two squares across and one square forward or back. This is the only piece that can 'jump over' other pieces.

QUEEN

Can move any number of squares in any direction.

CASTLE (also called ROOK)

Can move any number of squares forwards, backwards or across, but not diagonally.

PAWN

Can only move forward one square, except on the first move, when a pawn can move forward two squares. Pawns can only capture pieces by moving one square diagonally into the piece. They can never move backwards.

KING

Can move one square in any direction.

PERFECT YOUR SKILLS

If you want to be really good at something, you need to practise. Here are some tips to help you master your skills:

- **Repetition.** Some people say you need to spend up to 10,000 hours practising something in order to become an expert. That's a lot of repetition!

- **Reflection.** Think about what you're doing and how you're doing it, during and after your practice. What did you do well, what went wrong, and why? This will help you to improve next time. It can also be helpful to ask for other people's opinions of your performance.

- **Challenge yourself.** In order to get better you have to push yourself. Setting a target is a good way to do this – make sure the targets you set are achievable, but not without hard work.

THE
METEORIC
RISE OF
RAIN

SOUTH KOREA

The bright lights flashed and the bass boomed. The crowds cheered and screamed for their favourite star, Rain, to come on stage.

Three male dancers appeared and launched into a routine of smooth body rolls – but Rain was making everyone wait. The dancers suddenly stopped, their arms folded. The music got louder and a dark silhouette appeared on a podium – it was Rain. The screams became ear-splitting. He raised one arm and slowly sang the first line of his latest hit. The stadium went wild.

This was South Korea and Rain was a K-pop star. His singing was smooth, his dance moves electric – and he could fill huge stadiums with thousands of adoring fans.

HIS SINGING WAS SMOOTH, HIS DANCE MOVES ELECTRIC – AND HE COULD FILL HUGE STADIUMS WITH THOUSANDS OF ADORING FANS.

The two-hour show was sensational and Rain did two encores. Eventually, he had to say goodbye – although his fans would have happily watched him all night.

Backstage, Rain was filled with sadness that his mum wasn't there to see his success. As he sank into a chair in his dressing room and reached for a cold drink, Rain thought about her. What would she say if

she could see him now? She would be so proud of him.

Rain's mother had died when he was 18. Life was very different for him then. He wasn't even called Rain – his real name was Jung Ji-Hoon. His family were very poor, so poor that when his mum fell ill they couldn't afford the medical fees to treat her. They watched as she got sicker and sicker and eventually passed away.

As time passed, Rain wanted to achieve something in her memory. He wanted to become a K-pop star.

Rain had already been in a boy band and he practised his singing and dancing at every opportunity he could. He spent hours watching pop stars and learning their signature dance moves. Rain's work paid off and he joined a Korean entertainment company,

JYP Entertainment. Rain worked every day: dance routines, singing lessons, stage skills and more. Soon, his agents told him he was ready to go out to auditions to join a band. But he got rejected time and time again. The competition was tough, and Rain had to believe in himself to keep going.

Eventually, his hard work and talent paid off. In 2002, he released his first solo album, and his third album sold a million copies, topping charts in South Korea and throughout Asia. Since then, Rain has become a mega-star. He has sold out concerts from Tokyo to New York. He has released seven successful albums, starred in hit TV shows and acted in Hollywood movies. Singer, songwriter, actor, dancer and music producer, Rain has been named one of the '100 Most Influential People Who Shape Our World' several times by *Time* magazine. But Rain's ambition has always been the same – to work hard and do the best that he can, in memory of his mother.

RAIN

WHY SINGING IS GOOD FOR YOUR SOUL

- Singing causes chemical changes in your body – releasing endorphins, dopamine and oxytocin, which make you feel good.

- Singing with other people can have even more benefits, helping with anxiety and making you feel more relaxed.

- It teaches you to breathe better by using your diaphragm (the muscle across the bottom of your ribcage) and to breathe deeply. This also draws more oxygen into the bloodstream, improving circulation.

- Singing makes your throat muscles stronger, which can help to reduce snoring!

HOW TO BECOME A K-POP STAR

1. Audition for a top Korean entertainment company. Some pop-star trainees are only ten years old when they start.

2. If accepted, leave home to live and work with all the other young trainees.

3. Spend most of your time doing dance lessons, singing practice and acting classes. Expect ten-hour days – and you must fit your studies in, too.

4. Train for up to five years. Students who don't make the cut can be asked to leave at any time.

5. Hopefully, find success on stage as a solo K-pop entertainer or as a member of a boy or girl band ... But there are no guarantees in this business.

HOW TO SING BETTER

- Find out your 'vocal range'. Sing a note, then slowly go up to the highest note you can manage. Do the same again but down to the lowest note.

- Warm up your voice with 'lip trills'. Press your fingers on to your cheeks and blow out through your lips, making them vibrate. Then trill notes up and down.

- Singing uses lots of muscles in the face, neck and body. Pull faces, make different shapes with your mouth and stretch your arms out before you start.

- Take deep breaths and open your mouth wide when you sing.

- Record yourself. Listening to your own singing will help you to improve.

- Join a singing ensemble or a choir – or start your own group.

THE EXTRAORDINARY DETERMINATION OF

MALALA YOUSAFZAI

PAKISTAN

"Who is Malala?" shouted the masked man. He had just jumped on to a school bus. The bus was full – just ordinary girls on their way home from school. Nobody said a word, but some of the girls nervously glanced at Malala when the man said her name. The man knew immediately who she was. Seconds later, he pulled out a gun and shots fired out across the bus.

Malala fell from her seat on to the floor, covered in blood and unconscious. She had been shot in the head. One of the bullets had gone through her left eye socket and had narrowly missed Malala's brain. She was rushed to hospital for emergency surgery and the doctors weren't sure if she would survive. But, miraculously, Malala did and she was brought to Birmingham in the UK to get expert medical help to save her life.

Malala Yousafzai was born in Pakistan in 1997 in a place called the Swat Valley. In 2007, a group known as the Taliban took over the valley and new

"I TELL MY STORY, NOT BECAUSE IT IS UNIQUE, BUT BECAUSE IT IS THE STORY OF MANY GIRLS."

rules were put into place. They banned everyday things, such as listening to music and, at the end of 2008, they declared that girls could no longer attend school.

Malala couldn't believe it. Why was she not allowed to get an education? She was determined to keep going to school, even though it was very dangerous for her and her family.

ON 9TH OCTOBER, 2012, TWO MEN BOARDED MALALA'S BUS AND ONE OF THEM SHOT HER.

It is difficult to understand how an adult could shoot a schoolgirl aged only 15. These men were part the Taliban and they didn't like what Malala was doing. She had written a blog for the BBC about how difficult life was living under Taliban rule. It was called *Diary of a Pakistani Schoolgirl*.

After that, she became increasingly vocal in her criticism of how the Taliban were denying girls the right to an education. They wanted to stop Malala – so they decided to kill her.

SHE BECAME THE YOUNGEST PERSON EVER TO WIN THE NOBEL PEACE PRIZE.

Malala has done incredible things since recovering from her injuries, advocating human rights and also education rights for women. In 2014, she became the youngest person ever to win the Nobel Peace Prize. She gave an inspiring speech to the United Nations (UN) in New York on her 16th birthday, telling her story and speaking about the importance of education for everyone. What is even more amazing is that she did it in English, which is not her first language. Malala was clapped and cheered by people from over 100 different countries. The UN now celebrates her courage and tenacity with a special day on 12th July – 'Malala Day'.

HOW TO SPEAK In PUBLIC

Speaking out in public can be nerve-wracking, so try these tips:

- Prepare well so that you know what you are going to say. Write down notes on postcards if you're worried about forgetting anything.

- Practise as much as you can. Try on your own first, then in front of a friend or family member. You could even record yourself.

- Speak slowly, clearly and loudly enough for everyone to hear you.

- You could film yourself and watch it back to make sure you are talking clearly enough.

- A bottle of water is handy in case of a dry throat or cough.

- Remember that it's normal to have butterflies in your stomach before speaking in public. In fact, it might even help you give a better speech.

START YOUR OWN BLOG

A blog can be a good platform for sharing interests and getting your message out there. Here are some ideas to inspire you:

- Think of what you'd like to write about. Choose something you are passionate about, like reading, art or sport.

- Choose a name for your blog that relates to you or what you want to write about.

- How will you write your entries? You could start from your point of view, or interview friends and family and write about their opinions.

- Decide how regularly you want to post – weekly, monthly or whenever you feel like it.

THE FABULOUS FEATS OF PELÉ

> BRAZIL

A young boy ran around the corner of a dusty Brazilian street, kicking what looked like a ball with his bare feet. It was actually an old sock, stuffed with newspaper and tied up with string. But even without a proper football, anyone could see he had talent. He could do all sorts of skilful tricks, bouncing his 'ball' from knee to knee, on to his head and back. He had an obvious passion for the game.

The boy's name was Edson Arantes do Nascimento, but his friends nicknamed him Pelé. Though he was poor, and from a deprived neighbourhood called Bauru in São Paulo, this boy would grow up to become one of the best footballers – many would say *the* best footballer – in the world. The legendary Pelé!

Pelé was from Brazil, a country that adores football. And the day he was playing in the street – Sunday 16th July, 1950 – was the day of a very important match. The whole of Brazil thought that their team, the best in the world, were going to beat Uruguay in the FIFA World Cup at the famous Maracanã stadium. Everyone stopped working to watch the match. It was huge.

BUT THEN, THE UNTHINKABLE HAPPENED.

The score was 1–1 but, with ten minutes to go, Uruguay scored a second goal. Brazil had lost! Everyone was stunned. Men and women wept in the streets – Pelé's father was in tears. Pelé was nine years old and he was devastated. So he made a vow that he would never forget.

56

HE COULD DO ALL SORTS OF
SKILFUL TRICKS, BOUNCING HIS
'BALL' FROM KNEE TO KNEE,
ON TO HIS HEAD AND BACK.

"One day," he promised his father, "one day I will win you the World Cup." And that's exactly what he did.

At 11 years old, Pelé began playing for his first football team, Bauru. He was so good that, at 15, he was taken on as a player by Santos, a well-known Brazilian football club. By the time he was 17, Pelé had been selected to play for Brazil in the 1958 World Cup, an incredible achievement. This was his big chance to keep his promise.

Pelé's first goal of the tournament was sensational. It was in Brazil's quarter-final win over Wales, and he became the youngest player ever to score a goal in the World Cup. He followed up with a hat-trick in the semi-final against France.

Brazil were now in the final. Pelé didn't disappoint the cheering crowds.

He scored two spectacular goals against Sweden, and at the final whistle the score was Brazil 5, Sweden 2. Brazil were the winners. This was only the second World Cup to be televised and Pelé had shown off his incredible talent to the world. People were talking about him everywhere. He'd done it!

Pelé went on to win two more World Cups and scored an incredible 1,281 goals during his career. His ball control, dribbling and heading skills were legendary, but his famous move was the 'bicycle kick' – an acrobatic move in which, with his back to the goal, he jumped in the air and kicked the ball over his head into the goal. No wonder that, in 2000, Pelé was named Joint FIFA Player of the Century and Athlete of the Century by the International Olympic Committee.

HOW TO DO A KEEPIE-UPPIE

Bouncing a football on your knees, feet and head without letting it touch the ground is known as a 'keepie-uppie'. Use these techniques to perfect your skills. You could use a sock stuffed with paper to practise like Pelé.

1. Drop the ball in front of you and let it bounce once. Then use your foot to kick the ball up into your hands. Repeat this several times with each foot.

2. Now, make it a bit harder. Let the ball bounce, but instead of kicking it into your hands, kick it and let it bounce and then kick it again. Add as many bounces and kicks as you can without catching the ball.

3. Finally, start to leave out the bounce, so you can drop the ball, let it bounce once, then kick it twice before letting it bounce again. Build this up gradually until you don't need to bounce it at all.

You can use these skills with your feet, your knees, your shoulders and even your head.

HOW TO MAKE AN OBSTACLE COURSE

An obstacle course is a great way to practise your dribbling skills and is also very easy to set up.

1. Place five cones in a straight line at regular intervals. If you don't have cones, you can use anything you can find to create markers on the ground, like paper plates or saucepan lids.

2. A short distance away (leave plenty of space to run) place four more markers in a straight line parallel to the first, but in between the other markers, to make a zigzag.

The aim is to dribble the ball around each marker in a zigzag line from top to bottom. You can add more markers if you want to make it more complex.

TOP TIPS

- Remember to guide the ball with both feet

- Keep the ball close to your feet to remain in control

- Move the cones closer together to challenge yourself

- Time each lap and try to beat your times

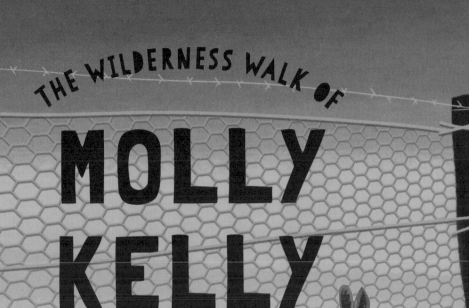

THE WILDERNESS WALK OF

MOLLY KELLY

AUSTRALIA

"No, not my granddaughters!" screamed the woman, trying to stop the policeman.

"Stop!" shouted the three girls, as they were bundled into the back of a car. The policeman told them to be quiet and slammed the door. Molly looked out of the window, tears streaming down her face, and saw her granny throw herself on the ground, crying. Then the policeman got in the car and drove them away.

Molly Kelly would always remember that terrible day, even when she was a very old lady. Before then, she lived with her family at a place called Jigalong on the edge of the Gibson Desert, Western Australia. Her mother was an Aboriginal Australian and her father was a white Englishman.

In 1931, when Molly was 14, she, her eight-year-old half-sister, Daisy, and their ten-year-old cousin, Gracie, were taken away from their home. They were driven to a place called the Moore River Native Settlement – a residence for mixed-race Aboriginal children. At the time, the

government believed that mixed-race children needed to be educated and trained to be able to integrate with the white Australian community. It was like a prison. Hundreds of children were taken away from their families. The windows had bars and children could be locked in their dormitories for up to 12 hours a day. The food was horrible – just bread, porridge and watery stew.

THE CHILDREN WERE PUNISHED IF THEY TRIED TO ESCAPE.

Molly was homesick and confused. She didn't know why she was in this awful place and she wanted her mother. So, after just two nights in the settlement, she decided to escape and walk home. But Australia is a huge country – and home was 1,600 kilometres away.

Molly didn't let that stop her. She persuaded Daisy and Gracie to go with her and together they escaped. Molly was clever. She knew that their home was built close to a very long fence that had been put up to keep rabbits out of Western Australia. This fence ran all the way from the north to the south of the country. If they followed it, they would eventually find their home in Jigalong.

Molly led the way and eventually they found the fence. They walked north, following the fence across the vast, hot Australian Outback. Molly knew some survival skills and she was able to catch rabbits to eat – and knew to avoid any dangerous snakes. They also found sweet potatoes and some fruits. But it was still very hard. They had hardly any water except for when it rained. Often the younger girls got tired and Molly had to carry them, but she never gave up.

The police were looking for them, but Molly made sure that they were not found. They walked for hours every day, rising early in the morning and not stopping until dusk. They crossed a river, sand dunes and a salt lake. And, nine weeks later, they finally came to the place they'd been looking for – home! Molly hugged her mum so tightly, she could hardly breathe.

It wasn't until 2008 that the Prime Minister of Australia officially apologized for the mistreatment of the Aboriginal people, in particular, the young children who were taken away from their homes. known as The Stolen Generations.

Molly will always be remembered for her incredible guts and determination, as the girl who walked 1,600 kilometres to get home.

WHAT HAPPENED TO HER?

Molly's amazing story inspired the 2002 film *Rabbit-Proof Fence*. She went on to get married and have two children. In 2004, Molly died at the age of 86 at her home at Jigalong.

HOW LONG UNTIL DARKNESS?

If you have no way of telling the time and need to know how long you have until darkness, you can use your hands to work it out.

1. Make sure no trees or clouds are blocking the sun or the horizon.

2. Hold one hand up horizontal with your palm facing you and your fingers together. Make sure your thumb is out of the way. Line up the bottom of your hand with the horizon.

3. Place your other hand above the first hand, with your palm facing you, your fingers together and your thumb tucked away.

4. Stack your first hand so it is above your second hand, making sure you keep your second hand still so you don't lose your place.

5. Continue to stack your hands until you have reached the sun. If there is still a little gap between your hand and the sun, use your fingers to measure the remaining gap.

6. Each hand represents 1 hour and each finger is 15 minutes. Don't forget to keep track.

OUTBACK FACTS

- More than two-thirds of Australia is covered by a vast area known as the Outback.

- Parts of the Outback are also known as the 'Never-Never' or the 'Back of Beyond'.

- The Outback is huge, dry and remote.

- Very few people live in the Outback – only 3 per cent of the country's population. Most Australians live in cities near the coast.

HOW TO SURVIVE IN THE OUTBACK

If you're travelling in the Outback today, you will usually be in a car.

Take lots of water. It can be very hot so you'll need about 4 litres a day.

Always tell someone where you are going, the route you are taking and when you expect to arrive.

If your car breaks down, stay with it. A car is much easier to find than a person.

Don't wander off the main road – it's very easy to get lost in the Outback.

- Stay in the shade and wait for help. Use as little energy as possible.

- If you run out of water, try to find a tree. If you tie a plastic bag over any leafy branches, water may collect in the bag.

- Look out for animal tracks that all lead to the same place – there may be a waterhole there.

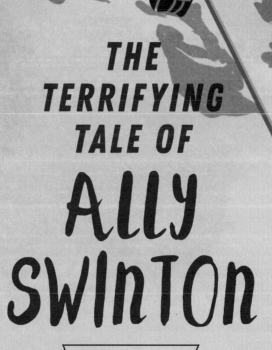

THE
TERRIFYING
TALE OF
Ally
SWInTOn

UK

Ally Swinton paused for breath. In the distance, he could see the dramatic sight of Mont Blanc – Western Europe's highest mountain peak.

An experienced mountaineer, 23-year-old Ally had already climbed Mont Blanc five times. Now he was coming down from the summit of a 4,000-metre peak that was close to Mont Blanc. Ally had gone ahead while his two friends were following behind him.

As Ally continued over the ridge, he felt relaxed and happy. He loved climbing and hiking, loved the challenge of getting to a summit and gazing at the amazing views. Deep in thought, Ally slipped on the glistening snow. *Woah!* he thought, as he landed on his side. *Be careful, Ally!* Luckily, he wasn't hurt. But what happened next was terrifying. As Ally lay there, looking upwards, he saw the snow above him crack and start to break up into gigantic pieces. Huge white slabs began thundering down towards him. An avalanche!

ALLY HAD SECONDS BEFORE THE MASSIVE WALL OF SNOW AND ICE HIT HIM.

He tried to keep calm and remember what he was supposed to do in this situation. So, he began to 'swim', doing a kind of front crawl to try to keep on top of the snow that was covering him. The power and force of the avalanche was unbelievable. As Ally was hurled down the mountain, tumbling around in a sea of white, his mouth and nose filled up with snow. Ally scooped the snow out, desperate to breathe, but more and more kept coming. *This is it*, thought Ally. *This is where my life ends.*

ALLY WAS SPEEDING DOWNWARDS AT A TREMENDOUS RATE.

He was thrown over a rocky ridge, then continued for a further 400 metres. Finally, the avalanche came to a halt. A shocked and bruised Ally found himself sitting among the snow and debris, with his backpack and equipment spread around him. He had survived!

Twenty minutes later, he heard his friends calling his name, then the glorious sound of a helicopter arriving to airlift him to safety. Ally knew he'd been very lucky – the avalanche could have thrown him on to the rocks on either side of him – but he had survived the 700-metre fall because of his quick thinking. Ally had literally swum his way to safety by keeping as close to the surface of the snow as possible. He had emerged from one of the most dangerous events that can happen on a mountain with only minor injuries.

His amazing story was in newspapers all over the world. Ally is a true survivor – one of the few people who have been hit by an avalanche and lived.

WHERE IS HE NOW?

Ally loves climbing as much as ever and is always challenging himself to reach new heights. He is always careful to take the correct safety equipment and to respect the mountains.

AVALANCHE!

WHAT YOU NEED TO KNOW

- Avalanches are hard to predict. Locals will know the times of year when an avalanche is most likely, so listen to their advice.

- Many avalanches are caused by people. A sudden movement, a sound or the weight of a person on unstable snow can trigger a slide.

- Be careful after heavy snow has fallen. If the sun is strong, it can melt the snow, causing a slide.

HOW TO SURVIVE

- Be prepared and take a device called a transceiver. This transmits an electronic signal that rescuers can pick up if you are buried in snow.

- An avalanche airbag, which inflates when you pull the cord, should prevent you from being buried.

- Try to avoid the avalanche by getting to one side of its path, or ski fast and veer away from it.

- Let go of any equipment or rucksack if you can, as it will weigh you down.

- If you are caught in a snow flow, stay as close to the surface as you can by making a front crawl swimming motion with your arms and legs. When the avalanche stops, you'll have more chance of getting out.

- If you are buried in snow, try to scoop out a breathing space around your face before the snow becomes solidly packed around you.

THE REMARKABLE LIFE OF
LIZZIE VELÁSQUEZ

USA

GRANDMA

SKINNY BONES

PORK CHOP LEGS

"Hey, Skinny Bones!" "Pork Chop Legs!" "Grandma!"

Five-year-old Lizzie could hear names being called as she walked towards her new classroom. She was confused. Who were these kids shouting at and why? She noticed that some of the girls and boys were staring at her and whispering. An awful thought came into her head. *Are they talking about me?* she wondered. Lizzie looked around. Everyone was looking at her. Suddenly, for the first time in her life, Lizzie realized that she was different from other children.

SHE WANTED TO LEAVE SCHOOL IMMEDIATELY.

Lizzie had been so looking forward to starting school. At home with her family and friends, Lizzie had never felt out of place or unusual. But at school, no one had ever seen a girl who looked like her. Some kids didn't want to play with her and others teased her. Lizzie would go home every day and cry her eyes out. Lizzie's parents told her to hold her head

high and ignore the names, but it was very, very hard.

Lizzie looked different because she had been born with a rare disease that meant her body could not process food properly. Because of this she was small and extremely thin. She had no sight in one eye and her features looked big on her face because of the illness.

As Lizzie got over her initial sadness, she realized school life also had its good side. She made some great friends, girls and boys who liked her and didn't care how she looked. With the support of friends and family, she got through her school years, studied hard and passed her exams, even becoming a cheerleader at high school.

But as Lizzie grew older, she had to deal with a new source of torment. On one of her worst days ever, when she was 17 years old, she found a video of herself on the Internet called 'World's Ugliest Woman'. She felt such pain and anger. How could people be so cruel? They didn't even know her! They didn't know how kind she was, or that she was funny and loved to laugh with her friends. They simply judged her because of her looks.

She understood that growing up did not mean an end to the bullying. Some adults who saw Lizzie's photo online posted cruel messages, saying that she should stay at home where no one could see her, even telling her that she didn't deserve to live.

Lizzie has faced a lot of challenges in her life. And she has learnt a lot from them. Experiencing other people's bad attitudes has made her want to be better than them. Lizzie realized one day that she had a choice – to decide whether to have a happy life or an unhappy life. It was all up to her. She decided to use her anger to prove the bullies wrong. She would end up the winner. And that's exactly what she has done. Lizzie dreamed of getting a college degree, writing a book and becoming a speaker who helps others with their lives. Through hard work, she has achieved all these things.

Lizzie is now an inspiration to many people around the world. She has stood up on behalf of many victims of bullying and proved that her experiences have given her the power to find kindness within. Her fans know how wise she is and they ask her for advice. Lizzie's message is always positive and stresses the importance of kindness and love. She knows that life can be hard, and sometimes disappointing, but with the right attitude, you can overcome these hurdles and be happy and kind. She has taken her life into her own hands and made it great.

WHAT IS BULLYING?

- Bullying is any behaviour that hurts another person. It can be physical – hitting and kicking, taking your things. Or it can be verbal – being mean, making threats, name-calling.

- Being ignored or left out is also a type of bullying.

- Bullies sometimes use social media to send photos and messages. This is called cyber-bullying.

- Bullying can happen anywhere, to kids or to adults – at school, at home, at work.

- If you're being bullied, always ask for help. Never keep it to yourself.

- Tell someone you trust, such as a friend, a teacher or a parent.

- It can be very hard to stand up to a bully. Sometimes it's best to walk away and find an adult to help you.

- If you are being targeted on social media, block the bullies and report the behaviour to an adult.

- If you think someone is being bullied, try to be a friend to them. This will let them know they aren't alone.

- Remember that this is not your fault. Nobody has the right to bully anyone else.

BEING KIND

1. Be considerate. Try to imagine how your actions and words might affect someone else.

2. Be aware of your friends and their behaviour. If you think they don't quite seem like themselves, ask how they are.

3. Be kind to yourself as well. Do things you enjoy that make you feel good.

MAKE A COMPLIMENT JAR

You can do this with a friend or on your own.

1. Cut 20 strips of paper.

2. Think of 20 nice things you like about yourself and write one on each piece of paper.

3. Fold the compliments and put them in a jar – a washed jam jar works well.

4. Decorate your jar with pictures and stickers. If you have a photo of yourself, why not glue it on top of the jar lid?

5. Screw on the lid and tie a ribbon around the neck of the jar.

6. Whenever you feel sad, take a compliment from the jar and read it to remind yourself how great you are. You will instantly feel better.

THE ASTONISHING ACHIEVEMENT OF LOUIS BRAILLE

FRANCE

Twelve-year-old Louis was bored – bored with school, bored with not being able to read or write, bored with everything. If only he could look at an interesting book or go for a walk on his own.

HE COULDN'T DO THESE THINGS BECAUSE HE WAS COMPLETELY BLIND.

Louis had been able to see perfectly when he was born, but at the age of three he'd had a horrible accident. He'd picked up one of his father's tools to play with – a pointed tool called an awl, used for punching holes. It slipped and hit Louis hard, right in the eye. Poor Louis developed an infection in both eyes and lost his sight completely. When he was older, he went to school in Paris, France, but it was a struggle. Louis always had to listen so hard and try to remember everything, because he couldn't read or write.

One day, an ex-soldier called Charles Barbier was visiting the school to give a talk. Louis thought that would be boring, too. But when Barbier started speaking, Louis pricked up his ears. Barbier was describing his invention of a special code for soldiers. When soldiers were on the battlefield at night, they weren't allowed to make a sound or strike a match for light, in case the enemy spotted them.

Barbier had worked out a way that the officers could tell the soldiers important things. He put raised impressions of dots and dashes on to paper to represent letters. If the soldier knew the code, he could 'read' messages silently in the dark, just by using his fingers to touch the patterns.

As Louis listened, he felt a tingle of excitement. Could a touching system like this help him – and others like him – to read? Louis got straight down to work.

HE FELT SURE THAT HE COULD CREATE A CODE THAT WAS MORE SIMPLE AND EFFECTIVE.

It wasn't easy. Louis decided to use only dots, in groups from one to six. He spent months trying to work out different arrangements that could represent all the letters of the alphabet. The dots needed to be small and easily felt with one finger. Louis used an awl – the same tool that had caused him to go blind – to punch tiny raised holes in paper. It took a long time to get it exactly right but by the time he was 15, in 1824, he had found 63 ways to use a six-dot cell in an area no larger than a fingertip.

By 1829 he had come up with a brilliant system. It worked for every single letter

and number, as well as musical notes, all kinds of punctuation, maths symbols – and more.

Louis Braille's system was named after him and now Braille has been used by blind and partially sighted people all around the world. Louis's hard work and clever thinking has enabled them to read books, newspapers, signs, do calculations and read music.

Louis Braille had played his part in opening up the world to millions of blind and partially sighted people worldwide.

HELEN KELLER

USA

At just 19 months old, Helen Keller contracted an illness that left her deaf and blind. When she was six, her parents hired Anne Sullivan, who taught Helen that objects have names, and then how to spell them using her fingers. Next, she taught her to lip-read by touch, to read Braille, to write and to speak. Helen was the first deaf-blind person to earn a Bachelor of Arts degree and she went on to become a successful author, political activist and lecturer.

BRILLIANT BRAILLE

Have you ever seen or touched Braille? Imagine these dots as tiny bumps. Just by touching each group of dots, you can 'read' the letters:

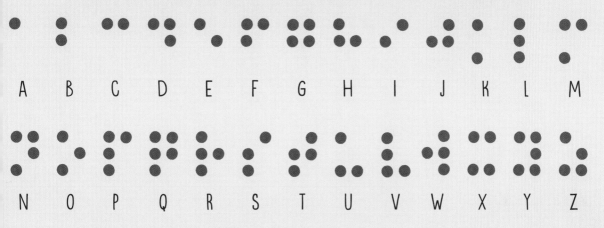

HOW TO SEND A CODED MESSAGE

THE CAESAR CODE

Each letter of the alphabet is represented by a different letter.

A	B	C	D	E	F	G	H	I	J	K	L	M	N	O	P	Q	R	S	T	U	V	W	X	Y	Z
D	E	F	G	H	I	J	K	L	M	N	O	P	Q	R	S	T	U	V	W	X	Y	Z	A	B	C

1. Write all the letters of the alphabet neatly in a row.

2. Underneath the letters, write the alphabet again, but start three spaces in, so that D is written directly under A, E under B, and so on. When you get to the end, use A, B and C under X, Y and Z. Now you're ready to send a message.

3. Write a message to a friend using letters from the second alphabet and see how long it takes them to 'decode' it.

Here's an example:

WKLV LV D VHFUHW PHVVDJH!

(This is a secret message!)

4. Make new codes by writing the alphabet again. This time, change the number of places you 'shift' the second alphabet. Or write numbers underneath the alphabet and use those instead. See if you and your friends can crack each other's codes.

THE SHOCKING STORY OF
BETHANY HAMILTON

USA

It was a perfect day for hitting the waves. Bethany Hamilton paddled out on her surfboard, happy and excited. She was at her favourite spot, Tunnels Beach, on the beautiful Hawaiian island of Kauai, with her best friend, Alana, and Alana's brother and dad. Bethany was only 13 years old and an excellent surfer – she'd been entering competitions since the age of eight.

SURFING IS A WAY OF LIFE IF YOU LIVE IN HAWAII.

Bethany lay on her board, relaxing as she waited for a big wave, her left arm dangling in the cool water. The sea sparkled in the sunshine – it was beautiful. Moments later, a dark shape under the water grabbed her arm violently, tugging her back and forth. Bethany gripped her surfboard tightly with her other hand,

trying to stay afloat. Then it was gone. A pool of red began to spread out in the water around her – blood. *I've been attacked by a shark,* Bethany thought.

She shouted for help. Quickly, Alana and her family swam over. In horror, they saw that Bethany's left arm had been ripped off just below the shoulder – and she was losing blood fast. Desperate to stop the bleeding, Alana's dad made a tourniquet out of a surfboard leash and wrapped it around the stump of Bethany's arm to try to stop the bleeding. Even though this probably saved her life, Bethany had lost over 60 per cent of her blood by the time she got to hospital.

SHE HAD GONE INTO SHOCK.

By chance, Bethany's father was already at the hospital. He was about to have an

operation on his knee, but Bethany took his place in surgery. The doctors sprang into action to repair the wound.

Later, investigators were shown photos of a 4-metre-long tiger shark that had been caught close to where Bethany was attacked. The shark's mouth was 43 centimetres wide – and its bite matched the marks on her surfboard.

BETHANY MADE AN AMAZING RECOVERY.

Some people might steer clear of the sea after such a terrible experience, but not Bethany. A month later she was back surfing, using a custom-made board with a special handle for her right hand. She had a tough time learning how to balance and control her surfboard with only one arm, but she never gave up.

Less than three months after the attack, she entered a major surfing competition. Since then, Bethany has excelled as a professional surfer, finishing in the top three in many competitions. Her courage and commitment has won her awards for bravery and the admiration of everyone around her. Bethany Hamilton is a true survivor.

HOW TO POP UP ON A SURFBOARD

1. Lie face down on your surfboard.
2. Place the palms of your hands in the middle of the board below you.
3. Push the top half of your body up.
4. Then quickly jump up, bringing your feet under your body so you are standing side-on to your board.
5. If you are right-handed, your right foot should be at the front of the board, and vice versa.
6. Your knees should be slightly bent.

HOW TO DEAL WITH SHOCK

Shock is a dangerous condition which happens when the body isn't getting an adequate flow of blood. Signs include:

- Cold, clammy skin
- Pale complexion
- Fast pulse and breathing
- Confusion and dizziness
- Nausea and vomiting

TAKE THE FOLLOWING STEPS:

1. Call for emergency help.
2. Lay the person down and raise their feet to increase the blood flow to the head.
3. Keep the person warm with a coat or blanket.
4. Do not let them eat or drink anything.
5. If the person vomits, turn them on to their side to prevent choking.

SHARK ATTACK! WHAT TO DO:

1. If you're close to the shore, swim away as quickly as you can and get out of the water. If you can't, stay calm and keep as still as possible. Don't splash about – the shark will think you are injured and grow more confident.
2. Try to get into a position where your back is protected by rocks, a reef or by another swimmer. That way you can defend yourself from the front.
3. If the shark attacks, hit it with a sharp object or your fists. Aim your blows at its eyes, gills or the end of its nose.

STAY SHARK SAFE

- Avoid surfing at night or dawn.
- Don't splash about.
- Look for 'Shark Warning' signs on beaches.
- Always surf in groups.
- Avoid murky water.
- Don't wear bright colours and patterns.
- Stay away from large groups of seals and fish, or anything that sharks eat.

THE CREATIVE CAMERA OF MOHAMAD AL JOUNDE

SYRIA

"Go on, have a look," said the photo-journalist, offering his camera to the boy. Mohamad took the camera and held it carefully in his hands. It was heavy. He'd never taken a photograph before. How did the camera work?

"I can teach you how to use it," said the man, whose name was Ramzi. He was a journalist who had come to the refugee camp where Mohamad was living to take pictures of the people there.

"Yes, please!" he said, excited. Ramzi was an excellent teacher and Mohamad learnt quickly. Soon he was out every day taking photos of the things around him. It opened his eyes to the world. Everything looked different and more interesting through the lens of a camera.

Photography quickly became very important to Mohamad. It was more than just a hobby to him – it was a way to express his feelings and to be creative. Mohamad hadn't had much chance to do either of these things. Two years earlier, he and his family had been forced to leave their home in Syria, when his mother's life was threatened during the war. Now they were living in the Bekaa Valley refugee camp in Lebanon and they had nothing. Mohamad had once had a nice home, a happy childhood and lots of school friends. Since arriving at the camp, he hadn't been to school for two years and his life felt empty and hopeless. He had nowhere to go and nothing to do. That was until the day he held a camera for the first time. Now he felt excited and full of ideas.

One day, Mohamad was watching the younger children wandering about in the camp. They looked bored and miserable.

Mohamad had made great friends with all the children. He had taught them how to use the camera.

What if taking photographs helped them too? he thought. He decided to give it a try.

A few months later, Mohamad had made great friends with all the children. He had taught them how to use the camera and they loved taking pictures. Mohamad realized that

many of the kids didn't want to talk about their lives or their painful experiences in war-torn countries. Taking photos of their surroundings and the people around them helped. It was fun, it was creative and it allowed them to express themselves. The kids learnt to trust Mohamad and he became their friend and teacher. He would play games with them, tell them funny stories and make them laugh. It felt so good to have fun again.

One thing that Mohamad missed a lot was school. There wasn't one in the camp, which meant that there was nothing for the kids to do all day. So Mohamad – aged just 12 – took matters into his own hands and set up one of his own. It started small – just a tent and a few children. Mohamed taught maths and photography to the younger kids and volunteers taught other subjects, such as English. With the help of his family, the school got bigger and eventually they had a proper building. Soon there were 200 children at the school learning every day with qualified teachers.

Mohamad knows how it feels to lose everything, to arrive in a strange new country and to have to start all over again. Through his love of photography, he set out to make a difference for children in the same situation. He has taught them creativity, confidence and how to enjoy being kids again. He wants everyone to know that education is the key to freedom.

WHAT IS HE DOING NOW?

Mohamad was awarded the 2017 International Children's Peace Prize for his work. He was given the prize by Malala Yousafzai, who won the same prize in 2013.

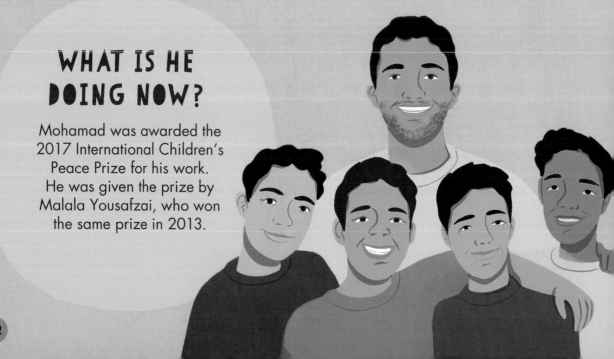

HOW TO TAKE AMAZING PHOTOS

YOU DON'T NEED AN EXPENSIVE CAMERA TO TAKE GREAT PHOTOS

1. Find something interesting for your subject. It could be a person, an animal, a building or an object. Go to a park for some great wildlife shots.

2. Think about where you want your subject to be in the photograph. It doesn't have to be in the middle – try the corner, bottom or top of the photo.

3. For a unique shot, take a photo from a different angle. Why not lie on the ground or take your shot facing up to the sky or down at the ground?

4. Think about light. The best light for taking photos is in the early morning and early evening. Take the same photo at different times of the day to see the difference.

5. Don't try to fill your photo with too much. Empty space around an object can really make it stand out. Your background could be sky, water, grass or a wall.

6. Be creative. Take photos with reflections in water, mirrors or glass. Experiment with shadow and light.

7. Take lots of photos. The more you take, the more you will see why some work better than others.

HOW TO BE A GOOD LEADER

Here are some tips for how you can act like a leader:

- Be confident and friendly.

- Make eye contact with people when you're talking to them.

- Stand up with your shoulders back — slouching will give a bad impression.

- Remain positive.

- Always look for solutions to your problems and act on them.

- Understand that everyone has different strengths and can contribute different things.

THE SUPERB SWING OF
PRATIMA SHERPA

NEPAL

"I won! Mum, Dad, I won!" cried Pratima, holding up her shining trophy. She had just won her first-ever golf tournament at the age of 11, beating 30 other competitors. Pratima's mother had tears in her eyes — she was so proud.

SHE HAD NEVER DREAMED THAT HER DAUGHTER COULD BE A GOLF CHAMPION.

Although golf was a big part of their lives, playing golf was not. Pratima's parents were workers at the Royal Nepal Golf Club. They spent their days cutting and watering the golf course so that the people who could afford to belong to the club could play.

Home for Pratima and her family was a shabby maintenance shed near the fourth hole of the golf course. It had no running water and they had to share the small space with the club's lawnmowers. Pratima was born in this shed, and she had been fascinated by golf since she was tiny. As a little girl she had watched the grown-up players and wanted to play golf just like

BY THE TIME SHE TURNED 17, PRATIMA HAD WON 33 GOLF TOURNAMENTS.

them. In the end, she climbed a tree, cut off a branch and asked her father to make it into a golf club for her. He carved it as best he could and made it roughly club-shaped. Pratima spent hours practising her swing with her home-made club, using golf balls that had been left on the course. She was very dedicated. Every day Pratima got up early, fed the family's goats and chickens, and practised golf before going to school.

EVEN DURING MONSOONS, PRATIMA WAS OUTSIDE PRACTISING.

People began to notice the young girl taking swings by the side of the course. They saw that she was gifted. One of the golf teachers was so impressed by her natural talent that he began giving her free lessons. Another club member gave Pratima a set of proper golf clubs.

In 2017, a family in the United States invited her to stay for a summer to play golf – so Pratima set off on her first trip away from home. She learnt a lot and has since gone from strength to strength. By the time she turned 17, Pratima had won 33 golf tournaments. She even had a private lesson with Tiger Woods, the famous US golf champion. Pratima had always been a huge fan of his and, through her hard work and commitment, her dreams were coming true.

The shed where Pratima and her family live is now full of her trophies – and she is one of the best female golfers in Nepal.

Opportunities for girls in Nepal are often quite limited, but Pratima is changing all that. She is determined to play golf for her country and to make it big in the international world of golf.

PUTT LIKE A PRO

1. Take your time. Plan the route you want the ball to follow. Keep an eye out for any lumps, bumps and slopes.

2. Get in position. Relax and stand sideways-on to the hole, with your weight evenly spread between your feet.

3. Take a steady grip of your club – firm but not too tight. Squeezing the club will make you tense your shoulders.

4. Don't flick your wrists or hands as you putt. Instead, make a smooth stroke from your shoulders.

5. Stay in control. It's easy to be over-enthusiastic when you're putting, especially if you're trying to hit the ball uphill. If you find that you're swinging your arms too much, try tucking a glove under your armpit that's closest to the hole, and keep it tucked

there while you make the putt.

6. Practice makes perfect. Stick two golf tees into the ground about 10 centimetres apart and try to putt the ball between them. This is often even harder than putting into a hole. When you've been practising like this, the holes out on the course will seem much wider.

CREATE A MINI PUTTING GREEN

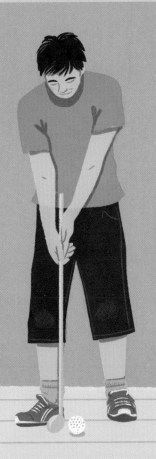

You can make a simple putting green to practise on at home. Here's how:

1. Find some outside or inside space where the floor is clear and there isn't anything breakable around.

2. Place some paper cups side-down on the floor. You could put a stone inside each cup to stop them moving around.

3. Try to putt the ball into the cups.

4. You could increase the distance between yourself and the cup to make the challenge harder.

KATHRINE SWITZER

> USA <

In 1967, Kathrine Switzer became the first woman to run the Boston Marathon – at the time, women were not allowed to compete. She registered with a gender-neutral name (K. V. Switzer), and managed to start the race without any problems. At around mile four, some officials noticed that a woman was running and tried to stop her, but luckily two other runners helped her get away so she could finish the race. Kathrine proved to everyone that gender didn't have anything to do with being a serious runner. Five years later, women were finally allowed to run the Boston Marathon officially.

THE INSPIRING LIFE OF
KEVIN BREEL

"And now – a new kid on the block. Please give it up for ... Kevin Breel!"

Kevin took a deep breath and tried to remember his first joke as he walked on stage. He felt so nervous. *Why am I doing this?* he thought to himself. It wasn't much of a stage – just a dusty old bar in a local hotel. The room was only half-full. But it didn't matter. Kevin reminded himself why he was here. He wanted to make people laugh. He wanted to smile and joke, and enjoy life again. Performing as a stand-up comedian was not only entertaining people – it was helping Kevin, too.

Seeing Kevin telling jokes that night, it was hard to believe that he suffered from depression. Just a few months before, he had come very close to ending his life because of it. Rewind to February, 2011, and 17-year-old Kevin was sitting in his bedroom, writing a note. He started with an apology to his mum and his sister. He was writing a goodbye letter.

Kevin tried to explain how he hated himself and felt that life was pointless. He wrote for a full half-hour, all his feelings tumbling out on to the page. By the time he'd finished, his hand ached and he was exhausted. But writing everything down helped Kevin realize what was making him consider doing this terrible thing. It was fear. *Am I really so afraid of life that I would rather die than face my fears?* he thought, his head in his hands. He began to cry.

KEVIN KNEW THAT HE COULD NO LONGER GO THROUGH WITH HIS PLAN.

Most people wouldn't have believed that Kevin was suffering from depression. On the outside, he seemed confident, funny and popular. But depression can happen to anyone, and Kevin became more and more afraid that people would see him for who he really was. He was scared to talk about it and his feelings of despair got

worse over the years. Until Kevin hit rock bottom.

THAT WAS HIS TURNING POINT.

Kevin knew he needed to get help and began seeing a counsellor. Talking about his depression was a game-changer. Over time, and with a lot of determination, Kevin slowly learnt to accept and love himself.

Since then, Kevin has left school and achieved his dream of becoming a comedian. He has also helped many people with depression. At 19, Kevin performed a TED talk called 'Confessions of a Depressed Comic'. Since it went online, it has become one of the most watched TED talks in history, with more than 4 million views. Kevin was named one of the most influential millennials in the world in 2015. What an achievement!

WHERE IS HE NOW?

By the time Kevin was 23, he was an award-winning comedian, mental health activist and writer. He hopes that his book, *Boy Meets Depression,* will help other young people like him.

TERRIFIC TED TALKS

A TED talk is a short but powerful speech, from anyone who's got an idea or a view that might help to change lives in a positive way. It is an online global community that is all about 'Ideas Worth Spreading'. TED stands for 'Technology, Entertainment and Design' but now covers almost all topics in more than 100 languages.

SO, YOU THINK YOU'RE A COMEDIAN?

- **The way you tell your jokes is key.** Practise your delivery with friends and family so you know when to pause and when to reveal the punchline. Timing is everything.

- **Practise an opener.** If you start your performance with a great line, you will have the audience hooked from the beginning.

- **Rehearse your routine.** Make notes to remind you of the order in which you want to tell your jokes.

- **Practise writing your own jokes.** Be inspired by the things around you and see if you can add a funny twist.

- **Find your own style.** Different comedians perform different types of comedy. Find the one that you like best and go from there.

HOW TO JOURNAL

Writing a journal can have lots of benefits. It can help you to work out your thoughts, you can be completely creative and you can spend as much or as little time as you like doing it. Here are some tips for where to start:

- You can make all sorts of journals, so think about what type of journal you would like to keep. It could be a gratitude journal, an ideas journal or just somewhere to write down anything that comes into your head.

- Find the right place to write your journal. You need to be able to relax and feel completely comfortable. It might be in your bedroom, in the library or even in a park.

- Choose the best time to write. You might like to do it before you start on anything else that day or you might prefer to reflect on your day before going to bed.

- Don't put pressure on yourself to write all the time. Find a way that works for you. It could be every day, every month or just whenever you feel like it.

- Remember, you don't have to just write. You could doodle, draw, scribble or anything else you feel like.

THE COLOURFUL CREATIONS OF FRIDA KAHLO

MEXICO

The wooden bus lurched to one side as it turned a corner. Frida and her boyfriend, Alejandro, held on to each other and laughed as they tried not to fall on to the seated passengers. Their smiles quickly turned to shock as they heard a loud crash. The bus shook and fell on its side, completely smashed open, with pieces of glass, wood and metal flying everywhere. There were awful screams and shouts for help. Something hit Frida in the stomach and she felt a terrible pain. Before she could scream, everything went black.

Days later, 18-year-old Frida opened her eyes. She was in a hospital bed. She couldn't move and her whole body hurt. The doctors told her that the bus she'd been travelling on had collided with a streetcar and several people had been killed. A steel handrail had pierced Frida's abdomen, fracturing her spine in several places and injuring her internal organs. Frida had broken her pelvis, ribs, right leg and collarbone, and her right foot was completely crushed. But she was alive.

Frida Kahlo had already faced many problems during her young life. Born in 1907 to a poor family just outside Mexico City, she had caught a disease called polio when she was six. This left her with a damaged leg and a limp. The bus accident caused Frida far worse injuries. She had to wear a body cast for three months after the crash and was in constant pain throughout her life. As a result, she had to spend a lot of time in bed.

HOWEVER, FRIDA NEVER GAVE UP HER DREAMS.

She had always wanted to paint, but she couldn't sit up or go outside to find interesting things to draw. One day, she realized there might be a way. She asked her mother to bring paints, brushes, a small easel and a large mirror. Her mother set the things up on Frida's bed where she could reach them. Frida saw her reflection – a striking, dark-haired young woman, wrapped in bandages. She was ready to start painting. As she had to stay in bed, she would paint the subject she knew best – herself.

Frida went on to become one of Mexico's most famous artists.

Her colourful paintings are known all over the world and are worth hundreds of thousands. One of her paintings sold for $8 million in 2016, and she has become an icon of Mexican identity and feminism.

Frida never gave up, even though she was always in pain. She loved being able to express her feelings through painting and she dedicated her life to art. Many of her paintings are self-portraits. They show Frida in lots of places – in bed, in a wheelchair, on a bus and even in her dreams. All of them are full of life and colour. Frida adored the bright colours of Mexico, dressing in vibrant clothes and wearing flowers in her hair. Frida Kahlo loved life, despite all of its hardships and challenges.

HOW TO DRAW A SELF-PORTRAIT

1. Start with paper, a pencil, a rubber and a mirror.

2. Look at your face shape carefully. Is it round, oval or long? Draw your face shape on to the paper.

3. Divide your face into four equal parts by drawing two dotted lines over it, one across and one down, in light pencil. This will help you to position your features. Notice how your eye line is actually at the centre of your head and not at the top, as you might have imagined.

4. Look closely at the size and position of your features and draw them on to the paper.

5. Remember that it might not be perfect the first time, so be prepared to make changes as you go along.

6. When you're happy with your features, rub out the dotted lines and add your ears, hair and neck.

7. Then you can get creative with colour.

BE CLEVER WITH COLOURS

- You can mix most colours from the three primary colours: blue, red and yellow.

- If you mix two primary colours, you get a secondary colour. Red and yellow make orange, blue and red make purple, and blue and yellow make green. The exact shade of the secondary colour depends on how much of each primary colour you use.

- If you mix two secondary colours, you get a tertiary colour.

- Complementary colours sit opposite each other on the colour wheel. If you use these colours next to each other, they create a vibrant contrast.

- Reds, oranges and yellows are warm colours. Blues, greens and purples are cool colours.

- White and black paint is useful for lightening and darkening other colours. Be sure to add just a little at a time.

- When mixing colours, remember that you only need a small amount of a dark colour to change a light colour, but you need a lot more of a light colour to change a dark colour.

- Be brave and experiment with colour! Look at other artists and see how they have put colours next to each other to achieve an effect. You can get some surprising results.

- Colouring books are a really fun way to experiment with different colours.

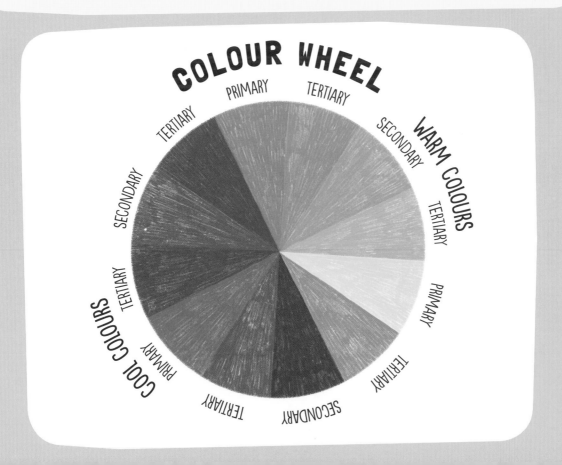

COLOUR WHEEL

PRIMARY · TERTIARY · SECONDARY · WARM COLOURS · TERTIARY · PRIMARY · TERTIARY · SECONDARY · TERTIARY · PRIMARY · COOL COLOURS · TERTIARY · SECONDARY · TERTIARY

THE SURVIVAL STORY OF THE
NONA SIBLINGS

Twelve-year-old Stephen was trying desperately to keep his head above the salty waves. He was treading water next to his sisters, Norita and Ellis. Their faces looked pale and scared as they bobbed up and down in the rough sea, doing their best to stay afloat. Nearby, their mum, dad and young brother were clinging on to the family's only life jacket.

"Swim over there!" their dad shouted, pointing towards a rocky outcrop. It seemed a very long way away. The siblings didn't want to leave their parents, but their dad insisted. He knew the three older children were good swimmers.

GETTING TO THE ROCK WAS THEIR ONLY CHANCE OF SURVIVAL.

"Come on," said Ellis, the eldest sister. "Let's swim. Quietly." They all knew that sharks lived in these waters and they didn't want to attract their attention. The three began swimming. Stephen turned around to see if his parents and brother were following, but they were still huddled in the water, clinging to the life jacket and holding on to each other.

Before the accident happened, the children had been in the boat, on their way to a birthday party with their parents. The family lived on Badu Island, part of the Torres Strait islands, which lie north of Australia. The party was on Thursday Island, a two-hour boat trip away. Halfway through the journey, disaster struck. The engine of their small dinghy failed and their boat was swamped by the waves. It capsized in the rough seas and the whole family were thrown into the water.

NOW THEIR PARENTS WERE GONE AND IT WAS TERRIFYING.

It was a long, hard swim and it was three hours before the children finally

reached the rock. It was tiny, no more than 4 metres wide. They clambered on to it and clung together, shivering as the sea crashed against its rocky sides.

For three days they waited to see if anyone was coming to rescue them. Being thirsty was the worst thing. There was no rain, no fresh water at all, and all they had to eat were some oysters they found on the rock. The children realized that they couldn't stay there any longer. They could see an island in the distance and knew they had to try to get there. "We have to swim – or we'll die," said Stephen.

Plunging into the sea, the three children swam towards the island. They set off in the morning and didn't get there until the afternoon. The island was deserted and only the size of a football pitch. But there was one palm tree. The children rushed to get the coconuts and tore the husks off with their teeth. After three days without water, the coconut water tasted so good.

Ellis, Stephen and Norita were stranded on the island for another three days, when suddenly they spotted something in the distance coming towards the island. It was their uncle in a boat. The children ran to him, crying, as he landed on the beach. They were hungry, thirsty and weak. But they had worked as a team, looking after each other and using their knowledge of the islands to help them against the odds. After surviving for six days on their own, they were hailed for their courage and bravery.

WHAT TO DO IF YOUR BOAT CAPSIZES

Your boat has capsized and left you in the sea without a life jacket. Here is what you need to do:

- The water might be very cold and could make you go into shock, which you need to avoid.

- Fight the urge to swim until your body has adjusted to the temperature. This will take up to 90 seconds.

- To do this, lie on your back and float until you can catch your breath. Move your arms and legs gently to keep yourself afloat if you need to.

- Your clothing can also help you float, as it traps air between layers as you fall into water. The less you move, the more air will stay trapped.

- When you have adjusted to the water temperature, you can start to signal for help or swim to shore.

- Remember to always wear a life jacket if you can.

MAKE A RESCUE SIGNAL

If you ever find yourself stranded or injured and in need of rescue, getting help should be a priority, and to do this you need to attract attention. Never make a rescue signal unless you really need rescuing though.

- A fire is a great way to attract attention. During the day, gather leaves, grass and damp wood to create a lot of smoke, and by night, burn drier wood to make the fire even brighter. Make sure you build your fire in a clear area away from dry grass and trees – you don't want to accidentally start a wildfire.

- Three fires arranged in a triangle is an international distress signal.

- You can also arrange objects on the ground, such as rocks, wood or any reflective materials that you can find, to spell out 'SOS' or to make a large triangle. This will help you alert a passing helicopter or plane.

- Use a torch or shiny object to reflect direct sunlight at the people or vehicle you are trying to attract. Three short flashes, three long ones, and three more short flashes spells 'SOS' in Morse Code.

HOW TO CRACK A COCONUT

1. The hairy outer layer of the coconut is called the husk. You need to pull this off.

2. At one end of your coconut you'll see three dents that look a bit like two eyes and a mouth.

3. Between the two eyes you should find a 'rib' or 'seam'. Follow this to the middle of the coconut and imagine a line that runs around its fattest part.

4. Use a rock to crack the coconut along this imaginary line – after a few taps it should break in half.

5. Smell the inside of the coconut before you eat any – if it smells mouldy or sour then don't eat it. Otherwise, you can drink the water and then you can use a sharp stone or shell to scrape out the white 'meat' and eat it.

THE SENSATIONAL SWIMMING OF
ELLIE SIMMONDS

Ellie shot through the water, face down, her legs kicking strongly, her arms propelling her forwards in a smooth front crawl. But this was no ordinary training session at her pool in Swansea, UK. She was in Beijing, China, swimming for the prize every athlete in the world wanted – a gold medal. She could hear hundreds of people cheering and shouting above the rushing of the water. *Keep going,* *come on Ellie, you can do this,* she told herself, her heart beating loudly. She was so focused that she didn't even notice the other swimmers in the lanes. Her only aim was to reach the pool wall, now only 20 metres away – the end of the race.

ELLIE TOOK A DEEP BREATH AND PUT EVERYTHING SHE HAD INTO HER LAST STROKE.

She touched the wall. It was over. A huge roar went up from the crowd. Ellie stayed in the water for a few seconds, panting, looking around to see who had won. She could see her supporters waving Union Jack flags, and could hear her name being announced – then Ellie realized what had happened. She had just won a gold medal at the 2008 Paralympics.

Ellie was in shock. She couldn't help the tears welling up as what she had just achieved dawned on her. She was only 13 years old and the youngest competitor in the British Paralympic team. She couldn't believe she had just won the 100 metres freestyle race.

All athletes have a hard journey, but Ellie's had been more difficult than most.

As a baby she was diagnosed with a condition called achondroplasia. This affected her bones and meant that she would not grow to average height.

BUT ELLIE HAS NEVER LET HER SIZE HOLD HER BACK.

She started swimming at the age of five and loved it. A few years later she was inspired when watching a Paralympic swimming race on TV. *I want to do that*, Ellie thought, when she saw the proud face of the winner that day. So that's exactly what she did. Ellie even moved to Swansea when she was 11 to get the best training. It was tough. Hours of pool training every day, before and after school. All her school work had to be done too, but Ellie was incredibly disciplined – the mark of a true athlete.

All that hard work paid off. Ellie went on to win a second gold medal in Beijing, for the 400 metres freestyle. Now everyone was talking about Ellie Simmonds. She appeared on TV and on the posters for the London Paralympic Games in 2012 – where Ellie again swam her way to two gold medals. More awards followed – the BBC Young Sports Personality of the Year Award in 2008 and an MBE from the Queen at Buckingham Palace. Ellie has made herself, and everyone in Britain, incredibly proud.

GET SWIMMING

Swimming is good for your heart and lungs, builds strength and helps you to keep a healthy weight. These tips will help you to become a strong and fast swimmer.

LOW BUBBLES

lowing bubbles helps eginners get used to having eir faces in the water – great r breath control. Stand in the ool, take a deep breath, put our face in the water, purse our lips and blow out stream of bubbles.

POOL TREASURE HUNT

Treasure hunting is good practice for diving down underwater and holding your breath. Ask someone to drop a swimming weight into the water and see how long it takes you to pick it up. Start at the shallow end and go deeper as you feel more confident.

UNDERWATER BRIDGE

Underwater bridges are a way to practise swimming underwater and controlling direction. Ask a friend to stand with their legs wide in chest-deep water, creating a 'bridge' shape. Swim through their legs and out the other side – without touching them. This might take a few tries.

HOW TO FRONT CRAWL

1. Swim face down along the top of the water, with your legs straight out behind you.

2. Use long, fast kicks. Your feet will make a small splash and your knees should be bent.

3. Move one arm at a time and lift them up, over your head, with your palms facing down.

4. As you pull your hand through the water when you reach back, you will propel forwards. Try not to splash too much.

5. Remember to breathe regularly. Turn your face to the side and out of the water when you take a breath.

SWIM TO WIN

- There are four main races in competitive swimming: backstroke, breaststroke, butterfly and freestyle.

- Freestyle means you can use any stroke that you like. Swimmers usually do the front crawl.

- There are lots of rules for Olympic and Paralympic swimmers to remember. For example, in a freestyle race, the swimmer's head must break the surface of the water at or before 15 metres from the start and after each turn.

THE SECRET LIFE OF
PIERRE DEMALVILAIN

FRANCE

"Stop!" shouted the German guard by the barbed wire. "What are you doing here, boy?"

Pierre turned around quickly. He'd been caught. His heart began to race. "I'm just looking for mushrooms, sir," he said, trying to look innocent.

The guard did not look convinced. "Come with me!" he shouted. "Move!"

Pierre was forced to walk with the guard towards the building that he had been spying on. He felt sick. Would the Nazis kill him? Suddenly, some German voices could be heard, and the guard looked panic-stricken. "Quick, hide in there," he said,

pushing Pierre behind a clump of bushes. The voices got louder and Pierre could hear the guard being shouted at. He was in trouble for leaving his post. Pierre peered through the thick greenery, trying to see as much as he could. He spotted German trucks concealed under camouflage nets and wooden crates that looked full of ammunition. *Very interesting,* thought Pierre, *this is a bomb depot.*

A few minutes later, the guard's face appeared through the leaves.

"GET OUT OF HERE!" HE HISSED.

Pierre breathed a sigh of relief. He ran as fast as he could to his bike, cycling away from what he now knew was a German

bomb depot. Pierre had completed his surveillance mission. It had been a close call and he'd been very lucky to escape, but it had been worth it. Pierre's discovery that day probably saved many lives. Great Britain was being heavily bombed by German planes and now the British Royal Air Force (RAF) knew where the bombs were being kept. They destroyed the hidden depot soon afterwards.

Pierre was 13 when the Nazis marched into his hometown, the port of Saint-Malo. It was June 1940, and Germany had invaded France. Pierre hated being under Nazi rule. It wasn't until he was approached by a mysterious man that he realized there was a way he could fight back. Pierre should have been in the shelters keeping safe, but instead he was watching the RAF from a vantage point. The man questioned Pierre. He wanted to know if he had a good memory, loved his country and could keep a secret. Pierre's answer to all these things was "Yes".

He started collecting information about the Germans. On 1st July, 1941, he officially joined the British-French-Polish Resistance network, known as F2. He was 14, and his secret life as an agent had just begun. Like all agents, Pierre had a special code name. His was 'Jean Moreau'.

Spying was dangerous work, but being young was a good cover. The Nazis didn't suspect Pierre – they thought he was just a boy out riding his bike. They had no idea that he was taking down details of German troops, vehicle number plates, tanks, planes and ships in his notebooks. Because he was good at art, Pierre made very accurate drawings of all the things he saw.

He secretly delivered his notes and diagrams to another Resistance agent, Raymonde, in Paris. Pierre would tell his parents he was going to a Boy Scout meeting every month and take the train to the city. Despite his bravery and courage in the face of danger, he could never tell anyone what he was really doing. Pierre was a true agent.

HE WAS 14, AND HIS SECRET LIFE AS AN AGENT HAD JUST BEGUN.

WHAT DOES IT TAKE TO BE A SPY?

- **Brave?** Spying is dangerous and you will find yourself in risky situations, possibly facing death.

- **Clever?** You will have to outwit your enemy and learn new skills fast. Speaking other languages will help.

- **Techie?** Modern spies use a lot of gadgets, such as bugs (electronic listening devices). Could you operate them?

- **Creative?** You'll need to think on your feet to get out of tricky situations and come up with good cover stories.

- **An actor?** Many secret agents have false names and identities. You must be totally convincing and never blow your cover.

- **Secretive?** Secret agents can't tell their family or friends what they do for a living. Could you keep a secret for years?

HOW TO CRACK A CODE

Follow these steps to work out how to crack a secret code:

- Look for any repeated letters or sequences of letters. Recurring patterns could help you to identify the type of code used.

- Look for short words, such as 'to', 'at' and 'I'.

- Write the message out backwards in case any words jump out at you.

- As soon as you have decoded a letter, write it down in capitals under the code.

- Swap the first and last letters of words in the code – a solution might become more obvious if you do this.

DEAD-LETTER DROPS

A 'dead-letter drop' is a safe and discreet way for spies to communicate. It means spies don't need to risk meeting in person. Follow these tips to set up a super-secretive dead-letter drop:

1. Think of a route you normally take – perhaps walking the dog or going to a friend's house. No one will be suspicious of you heading off somewhere that you usually go.

2. Wrap your message in a plastic bag so it stays completely dry.

3. Choose a discreet place to put your letter. Surprisingly, it can be better to carry out a dead-letter drop in a busy place, such as a park or café, than an isolated location where you will stand out.

THE FEARLESS FIGHT OF
JULIANA OSSA

USA

Ten-year-old Juliana walked over to the lake and dipped her toe into the water. It was a hot, sticky day in Florida, USA. She and her family were at a beauty spot called Moss Park in Orlando, a popular place for locals and tourists to visit. Juliana stepped into the inviting water and enjoyed its coolness. She paddled for a while, then sat down in the shallow water to relax, her legs in front of her. It was quiet, and Juliana felt calm and peaceful.

AS SHE DAYDREAMED, SHE FELT A SUDDEN, SHARP PAIN IN HER LOWER LEG.

Startled, she looked down into the water to see a large, dark shape alongside her.

Whatever it was had got hold of her leg and was biting her – hard. It was an alligator.

Juliana couldn't believe her eyes. She hit at the creature with her fists, but the alligator kept on, gripping her leg tightly with its huge jaws. It wasn't letting go. But Juliana didn't panic. She had suddenly remembered something. A recent visit to Gatorland – a local wildlife reserve with hundreds of alligators and crocodiles – had taught her all about these dangerous creatures. The instructor had told the visitors what to do if an alligator attacked.

Go for its snout. She took a deep breath and, as hard as she could, rammed her fingers up the alligator's nostrils. It felt horrible. But it worked. The alligator had to let go of Juliana's leg in order to open its mouth and take a breath.

As it released her from its grip, Juliana's panic-stricken step-uncle came running over and pulled her out of the water to safety. He carried her to a nearby picnic table and the emergency services were called. Juliana was in shock.

> SHE LOOKED DOWN
> TO SEE BLOOD STREAMING
> FROM HER LEG.

When the paramedics arrived, they treated her injuries and she was taken to hospital. Juliana had puncture wounds on her left knee and lower thigh from the vicious attack – she was lucky to be alive. The paramedics who helped her said she was extremely brave and very calm. Her quick-thinking had helped to save her life. She had remembered – and used – the advice she'd been taught.

The park rangers later found the alligator that had attacked Juliana. It was 2.6 metres long – a real monster. Juliana's terrifying tale and incredible bravery made newspapers and TV reports all over the world.

CROC' OR 'GATOR?

THEY MAY LOOK SIMILAR, BUT HERE'S HOW TO TELL THEM APART:

The snout: Alligators have a wide U-shaped snout. Crocodile snouts are V-shaped and narrower.

The teeth: You generally can't see an alligator's lower teeth when its mouth is shut. With a crocodile, you can often see its bottom teeth, especially the large fourth tooth.

Location: Alligators prefer freshwater sites while crocodiles are normally found in saltwater areas.

Colour: Alligators are usually dark grey or black in colour. Crocodiles are a lighter brown or green.

REMEMBER, REMEMBER

It can be hard to remember useful information, but sometimes it can be life-saving.

- **Take notes.** Then you can re-read them whenever you need to.

- **Exercise your mind.** The more you practise using your brain, the better it will be at remembering things.

- **Use mnemonics.** This is when you attribute the first letter of each word to another meaning that will help you remember a sequence.

MNEMONIC

This example might help you recall the continents:

North America	Never
Europe	Ever
South America	Smile
Africa	At
Asia	An
Australia	Angry
Antarctica	Alligator

ALLIGATOR ATTACK!

DOS

- If you can escape, run. Alligators are fast, but they can only run for short distances.

- Hit the snout, its most sensitive part, and, if you can, try to block its nostrils.

- Try to gouge the alligator's eyes, which are another sensitive part of its body.

- Make as much noise as possible. Many alligators will run away if you scream and shout a lot.

DON'TS

- In areas where alligators live, don't paddle or swim in the water.

- Be especially careful after dusk, when alligators are out hunting for food.

- The best way to stay safe is to keep away from their territory.

THE TUNEFUL TALE OF
SHEKU KANNEH-MASON

<< UK >>

Sheku's eyes widened as the music came to an exhilarating finale. He was just six years old but, from that moment on, he knew he had to play the cello.

His older sister and brother already played instruments, and hearing them practise made Sheku desperate to start his own musical adventure. He loved the sound of the cello so much that he didn't ever want to put it down – he was always playing and practising. As a result of all this dedication, he passed his Grade 8 examination with the highest score in the country when he was only nine years old.

IT WAS JUST THREE YEARS AFTER HE FIRST STARTED PLAYING.

As one of seven children who all played instruments, it was very expensive for his parents. Sheku practised for hours each day. Sometimes his dad would even wake up and hear Sheku playing in the bathroom on a Sunday morning. He worked so hard that he won a scholarship to the Royal Academy of Music, in London.

Then an instrument maker lent Sheku his first full-size cello, which would have cost thousands of pounds to buy. There was no way his family could have paid for it. Sheku began getting up at 4:30am every Saturday morning, so he could get a train from his hometown of Nottingham down to London for his cello lessons at the Royal Academy.

When Sheku was 16, ten years after he first decided to become a cellist, he entered the 2016 BBC Young Musician of the Year competition. It would soon change his life. He made it through all the rounds to the final. This was going to be one of the toughest performances of his life – not only was it mentally draining, but it was physically challenging as well. He had been practising for a long time, but he knew he had to be calm and focused when he walked on stage. It was a tough competition. The most talented young musicians from all over the country took part and Sheku knew they had all performed to the highest standard.

Sheku gave the best performance he could, playing Cello Concerto No. 1 by his favourite composer, Shostakovich. After the very last note, he took a breath and looked up to see the crowd cheering and clapping.

Waiting for the judges' final decision was so nerve-wracking.

"AND THE WINNER IS ... SHEKU KANNEH-MASON". THE CROWD ERUPTED.

Since then, Sheku has continued to play, and was even asked to perform at the wedding of Prince Harry and Meghan Markle. He is now a full-time music student and he knows that his success was down to the fact that he had access to music as a child. He has donated £3,000 to his old school to help fund cello teaching. Today, he enjoys his small concerts just as much as his big ones, because playing for children in schools gives them the opportunity to experience music like he did. He is dedicated to inspiring young children to play musical instruments.

PRACTICE MAKES PERFECT

Learning to play an instrument takes time and practice. Here are some tips for how to practise like Sheku:

- Slow everything down, so that you're playing in tempo but at a much slower pace.
- Record yourself so that you can listen back. This will help you to evaluate your playing.
- Make up your own practice exercises to warm up.
- Listen to the pieces you are learning being played by other people to help you to understand the music.

ORCHESTRA KEY:

1. Violin
2. Viola
3. Cello
4. Double bass
5. Harp
6. Xylophone
7. Timpani
8. Bass drum
9. Snare drum
10. Castanets
11. Gong
12. Grand piano
13. Cymbals
14. Trumpet
15. Tuba
16. Trombone
17. French horn
18. Cornet
19. Flute
20. Piccolo
21. Bass clarinet
22. Clarinet
23. Cor anglais
24. Oboe
25. Bassoon
26. Contrabassoon

INSTRUMENTS

THE HIGH-FLYING LIFE OF
AYESHA FAROOQ

PAKISTAN

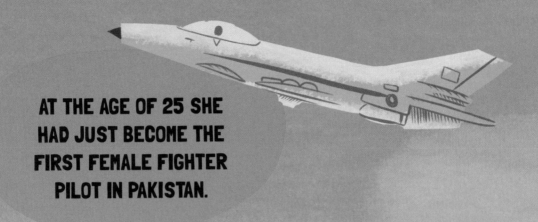

AT THE AGE OF 25 SHE HAD JUST BECOME THE FIRST FEMALE FIGHTER PILOT IN PAKISTAN.

Ayesha said a little prayer to herself as she sped down the runway and took off. She was flying on her own for the first time, with no instructor watching her or telling her what to do.

I'M IN CHARGE, SHE THOUGHT TO HERSELF. I'M IN CONTROL OF THIS AIRCRAFT.

The aircraft in question was an F-7PG fighter – a sleek, hi-tech jet plane. And Ayesha had good reason to congratulate herself. At the age of 25 she had just become the first female fighter pilot in Pakistan. This was her dream job, and she had earned it after years of hard work.

Ayesha Farooq was brought up in Bahawalpur, Pakistan. Most girls living there would not even consider a career as a pilot, but Ayesha was different. She wasn't interested in playing quietly indoors, preferring to go outside to play football and cricket. Her father had died when she was three, and Ayesha and her younger sister were brought up by their mother. Her mother raised them to be strong – this gave Ayesha the confidence that she could overcome the challenges she would face. There was never any doubt in her mind that she would become a pilot like some of her uncles and her cousin, who were officers in the Pakistan Air Force. However, her uncles did not agree. Surely being a pilot was a man's job?

Ayesha knew this wasn't the case and she was determined to achieve her dream. So, after finishing school, she applied to the Pakistan Air Force Academy for pilot training. There were lots of difficult tests, but Ayesha passed them all and then began her training properly. It was tough.

Every morning the trainee pilots would wake up at 4:30am to go for a run. They had to carry heavy guns for hours. They learnt how to eject from the plane in an emergency and how to survive a crash-landing in water and on land. And, of course, they learnt how to fly a fighter jet. This involved a huge amount of technical skill, as pilots must become experts at controlling their plane and using its weapons. All fighter pilots must be ready to go to war if their country needs them. It was so rare for women to complete this training that some of the training bases didn't even have women's toilets.

In 2013, Ayesha qualified and became Flight Lieutenant Ayesha Farooq. This was a huge achievement in a country where many girls don't even go to school. Thanks to women like Ayesha, things are slowly changing for girls in Pakistan. The country now has over 300 women in its air force, though very few are pilots.

Ayesha always wanted to prove that women and men could do the same job, and now she has become a role model for young girls, who call her up and ask her how to become a pilot. She is always delighted to tell them how she did it.

SO, YOU WANT TO BE A PILOT?

Here are some of the skills you will need:

- Be good at maths and physics.

- Understand how an aircraft works.

- Be good at communicating.

- Have excellent eyesight and hand-eye co-ordination.

- Enjoy leading and being part of a team.

- Be able to think quickly and make decisions under pressure.

PROCEDURE WORDS

Procedure words are used to communicate via radio. Here are some good terms to know:

Mayday: Help

Roger, out: Signals the end of the conversation

Ten-four: Confirms that you understand the message

Sit-rep: Stands for Situation Report, for when you need to know where someone is or if they are hurt

SPEAK LIKE A PILOT

The NATO phonetic alphabet is used all over the world so that people can communicate in a way that is understood by all.

Alfa	Juliet	Sierra
Bravo	Kilo	Tango
Charlie	Lima	Uniform
Delta	Mike	Victor
Echo	November	Whiskey
Foxtrot	Oscar	X-ray
Golf	Papa	Yankee
Hotel	Quebec	Zulu
India	Romeo	

FOLLOW YOUR DREAMS

- Make a list of what you want to achieve to help you to determine what your goals are.

- Set big, bold goals but break them down into smaller tasks so they are achievable.

- Be aware of procrastination – don't let yourself get distracted easily.

- Ask for help. Friends and family might be able to offer you invaluable advice.

- Be determined and don't give up. You might face some challenges, but don't let them stand in your way.

FOR THE EXTRAORDINARY NIA AND RHIAN YATES!

Every reasonable effort has been made to represent these stories accurately. Any errors or omissions that may have occurred are inadvertent, and anyone with any queries is invited to write to the publishers, so that amendments may be included in subsequent editions of this work.

WARNING: Many of the situations in this book have inherent dangers and can lead to serious or even fatal injuries. Readers should not venture into any of these situations without professional instruction, suitable training and proper supervision.

The publisher and the author disclaim all liability, as far as is legally permitted, for accidents or injuries or loss of any nature that may occur as a result of the use or misuse of the information and guidance given in this book. Above all, exercise common sense, particularly when fire or sharp objects are involved, and follow at all times safety precautions and advice from responsible adults. That said, it is fun to learn new skills, and they may one day be useful.

First published in Great Britain in 2019 by Buster Books, an imprint of Michael O'Mara Books Limited, 9 Lion Yard, Tremadoc Road, London SW4 7NQ

 www.mombooks.com/buster

 Buster Books

 @BusterBooks

A CIP catalogue record for this book is available from the British Library.

ISBN: 978-1-78055-578-2

1 3 5 7 9 10 8 6 4 2

This book was printed in July 2019 by Leo Paper Products Ltd, Heshan Astros Printing Limited, Xuantan Temple Industrial Zone, Gulao Town, Heshan City, Guangdong Province, China.